Seeking God in All Things
Theology and Spiritual Direction

William Reiser, S.J.

A Michael Glazier Book

LITURGICAL PRESS
Collegeville, Minnesota

www.litpress.org

Cover design by Greg Becker. Photo by Gettyimages.

1   2   3   4   5   6   7   8

Library of Congress Cataloging-in-Publication Data

Reiser, William E.
   Seeking God in all things : theology and spiritual direction / William Reiser.
     p. cm.
   Includes bibliographical references and index.
   ISBN 0-8146-5166-6 (pbk. : alk. paper)
   1. Spiritual direction. 2. Catholic Church—Doctrines. I. Title.
BX2350.7.R45 2004
253.5'3—dc22   2003020272

For, as I have said, the mind of humankind cannot remain constantly in the same state, nor will any holy persons, while living in this flesh, possess the height of the virtues in such a way that they will abide unchangingly. For something must always be either added to them or taken away from them, and no perfection will exist in any creature that is not subject to passion or change.

—John Cassian, *The Conferences*

"You have made me so rich, oh God, please let me share out Your beauty with open hands. My life has become an uninterrupted dialogue with You, oh God, one great dialogue. Sometimes when I stand in some corner of the camp, my feet planted on Your earth, my eyes raised toward Your heaven, tears sometimes run down my face, tears of deep emotion and gratitude. At night, too, when I lie in my bed and rest in You, oh God, tears of gratitude run down my face, and that is my prayer. I have been terribly tired for several days, but that too will pass. Things come and go in a deeper rhythm, and people must be taught to listen; it is the most important thing we have to learn in this life. . . . Sometimes I try my hand at turning out small profundities and uncertain short stories, but I always end up with just one single word: God."

—Etty Hillesum, Letter from Westerbork, 18 August 1943

For surely I know the plans I have for you, says the LORD, plans for your welfare and not for your harm, to give you a future with hope. Then when you call upon me and come and pray to me, I will hear you. When you search for me, you will find me; if you seek me with all your heart, I will let you find me, says the LORD.

—Jeremiah 29:11-14

Contents

A Personal Preface

On a bright morning in late spring of last year, I had set out to mow the grass. A youngster on the way to school paused to look at the lawn and spotted tiny purple sprinkles. After informing me about how pretty the flowers looked, she asked if I intended to spare them. Well, I explained, that would be rather hard to do. Violets, after all, were awfully small and they had sprouted all through the tufted grass, which badly needed mowing. "Oh," she answered. And then after surveying the yard for a second or two, she asked, "Well, do you really need to cut your grass today?"

All at once the gospel text about wheat and weeds blew through my ears. Spare the violets, spare the wheat: in tearing out the world's weeds we may rip up the grain. But the innocence of her concern pointed my imagination in a different direction. The grass was to be my morning project. Afterwards I would savor the completion of a neat, manageable task—a consolation all the more welcome because much of my life seems to drag along in a chronically untidy, unfinished state. The little girl's "Do you need to cut your grass today?" came from her anxiety over the fate of the violets; the color and sheer randomness of beauty had caught her eye. Is it possible, I was wondering as the mower went about its job, that life has turned into a series of chores and projects—as if I were living on an allowance and hours had become my quarters? Maybe. Yet I also realized that the divine eye is, mercifully, far more attentive to flashes of color than the eye of our best artists. Whenever life starts to feel like a vacant lot overrun by weeds, it's important to recall that weeds are hardly the whole picture. Little by little we can lose our ability to notice the flecks of color that dot the landscape.

I meet many families whose religious needs are only occasional; their ties to the church are real but thin. Although they have an awareness of

God, they have little evidence that God would be particularly interested in them. The prospect of spiritual direction would be the furthest thing from their mind. When it comes to helping such people, it's pretty hard to assess success. I've been doing some hard thinking about that lately—the result, I suppose, of having more years behind me than ahead. It would be relatively easy to give an accounting of one's stewardship by listing the things one has done, but a list of good deeds does not necessarily reveal what we have actually accomplished. Who of us knows how something we may have said or done has helped others as they struggled for greater self-control, or patience, or compassion, or more fervent prayer? Actual graces—the innumerable, ordinary ways God reaches into our lives—someone's courtesy and attentiveness, for example, or a friend's honest words, the embrace of forgiveness, or the memory of our parents praying—are often too subtle for us; we might not even realize that we've received them. Yet we are constantly acting upon one another for good. Even loved ones who have died touch us, through the wonderful capacity we have for remembrance.

When I ask myself, then, what I've accomplished in my life, not what I've done, I'd have to answer quite honestly that I don't rightly know. Yet anybody involved in the care of souls would probably make the same admission. The enduring fruit of the investment we make in each other as spouses and parents, as sisters and brothers, as companions and coworkers cannot be measured in material terms. Indeed, how could the final disposition of any life come to light until God sifts us clean? People may recall a preacher's sincerity, a celebrant's piety, a spiritual director's attentiveness far better than any words spoken. What people take away from our preaching, direction, and instruction—like readers leaving notes in the margins of books—would probably astonish us by its dissimilarity from what we intended to say. The process of salvation reveals a lot more happenstance than intention or design, almost as if we're destined to discover God by accident. For most of us, I believe, life's lasting accomplishment is going to consist of how much of our selves we managed to impart to one another. And since that's a process only divine eyes can see, it must also be the thing about us which most gives God glory.

In the classroom I'm surrounded by young people of great promise—intelligent, devout, idealistic, and eager to step into a complex and challenging world. Walking Main Street toward downtown, I'm in the midst of a reality altogether different. Two teenagers had ducked into a doorway, the pungent, sweet smell of marijuana trailing them as they braced against the jamb. How many grades had they repeated before giving up on school? My mind raced ahead to the social calamity likely to be their legacy, and then backwards to the home life they had almost certainly come from. One afternoon a woman alighted from a car right out front, as if she lived here. Then leaning inside the back seat, she kissed two children. She waved to them as the car drove off and walked to her spot at the corner, waiting for a customer.

Such scenes don't fade and disappear. We may forget why we went into the kitchen, but let's hope we don't forget the voices and faces—and the hands—of the people whose social world at one and the same time is both unbelievably close and terribly far away. In another age some of them would have been driven by curiosity and desperation—and the invitation of an angel—to make their way toward Bethlehem. What an image: the poor and the misfits trailing an angel and the rest of us following them to the place where the Savior is born.

You must certainly be thinking that this is an odd way to begin a book on the theology underlying spiritual direction and I readily concede you may be right. But a writer's orientation and location are helpful clues when it comes to figuring out what he or she may be trying to say. In thinking about spiritual direction, I find myself thinking about how God reaches into human lives; as soon as I step outside the front door I begin to notice an awful lot of lives where God, at least to my eye, doesn't seem to be all that present. Worcester, Massachusetts, is hardly the Bronx; yet as I was reading Adrian Nicole LeBlanc's *Random Family*, I felt I had a pretty fair grasp of the lives she writes about. Spiritual direction, at least as many of us have come to think of it, seems just plain irrelevant to the sort of people that in my imagination surrounded Jesus. Come to think of it, I doubt that a spiritual director accompanied Francis Xavier to the Indies or that Jesus had one in the wilderness. But when I think of spiritual direction as part of the ministry of catechesis, the practice of direction no longer seems to me to be elitist or restricted to people of cultural privilege. And when I think about the theology of spiritual direction in conjunction with my preoccupation about how God is going to save people who are just barely surviving as human beings, my mind drifts quickly to the narrative world of the Gospels. The one gospel story where Jesus comes closest to accompanying someone spiritually, for me, is the scene where he meets the distraught father of an epileptic boy. For in that story Jesus grasped how the family's constant anxiety and fear had just about pulverized their faith in God—and then he speaks with the father from the depths of his own tested faith. "All things can be done for the one who believes" (Mark 9:23). That's not pious reassurance; that was experience speaking. In the process of spiritual direction faith reaches out to faith, and both of us grow as a result. The father of that epileptic child would not be at all interested in the questions I am asking in this book, but on the other hand if it were not for people like that father I would never have come to the conclusions I have. Being-with-Jesus makes his followers distinctive in far more ways than we might imagine.

And so, one's ideas and one's everyday experience connect. I can't think about spiritual direction without recalling the faces I pass on the street, I can't walk by one of the many tiny evangelical churches without thinking of the minarets and stupas I've seen in the Far East, I can't read Paul's words about salvation without thinking of lives cut short by drugs and violence and how I once watched those same kids play basketball on the lot outside the kitchen window. Even the potholes—those annoying legacies of winter—that force me to avoid shortcuts and modify my driving pattern become premonitions of what being a Christian might be like in a politically unfriendly world. Where our feet are and where our heads are, what we think about and where we're located socially, mind's eye and physical setting are inextricably tied together.

Two years ago it struck me that when prayer is only a matter of talking to ourselves it soon becomes boring and tedious; but when in talking to ourselves we have the happy awareness that God is listening, the praying feels refreshing and liberating, like someone breaking out of a large paper bag. I owe that insight to the remark of a four-year-old. She had been talking to herself and her mother overheard. The little girl scolded her mother, "You shouldn't be listening to other people's conversations!" I thought to myself, it's not that I talk or that God merely overhears, but that I am aware of God's overhearing, which spells the difference between tedium and excitement. When it comes to thinking about our relationship with God, who knows where the insights will come from?

I should like to add a word about words. Readers and writers alike have grown increasingly sensitive to the limitations of language when it comes to speaking about the divine mystery, particularly language that genders God. For most of us the primary sources of religious rhetoric and imagery have been the Bible and the Liturgy, and there the divine mystery is personalized. Avoiding personal pronouns altogether in referring to God can make some sentences sound flat. Using the masculine forms turns some readers off right away, while alternating masculine with feminine pronouns and adjectives does little to improve things—not because the feminine experience of God has no theological standing but because the wording then seems not to be congruent with the scriptural and liturgical phrasing our ears have grown accustomed to. The fact that the Bible uses masculine pronouns hardly means that God is masculine any more than it should imply that God is human. If we were to substitute feminine pronouns we would certainly be drawing attention to the fact that there has always been a feminine experience of God and a feminine side to the divine self-revelation in Scripture. But the fact that we use pronouns at all does not give us permission to conclude that human nature or personhood can be a predictor of the form of God's being. To some ears (my own included) the word "god" itself has a frosty ring to it; the word sounds faceless. As a result, I have trained myself to hear "divine mystery"—a phrase that at least for me has a bit more complexion—whenever the word "god" is written or spoken, and I suspect that many people have come to make similar substitutions. Biblical and liturgical texts play a key role in the formation of a fully ecclesial faith, yet there are other many determinants—cultural, social, geographic, historical—to a person's religious experience. Hence the need for sensitivity. In our religious tradition the divine mystery is hardly faceless, but neither is it a supremely magnified version of the human heart.

The reader will probably notice the influence of Mark on my thinking about the spiritual life. A number of the perspectives developed here continue the sort of reflection I undertook in *Jesus in Solidarity with His People: A Theologian Looks at Mark* (The Liturgical Press, 2000). Throughout the book I have generally used the New Revised Standard Version of the Bible (NRSV), but on occasion I draw on the Revised Standard Version (RSV), the Revised English Bible (REB), the Jerusalem Bible (JB), the New International Version (NIV), and the New American Bible (NAB). My own Jesuit roots and vantage point will be apparent throughout this book. Ignatius is, of course, St. Ignatius Loyola; the "Exercises" are his *Spiritual Exercises*.

I am grateful to Joel Villa and John Buckingham of Audio-Visual Services at Holy Cross College for their help in photographing and editing the two illustrations that appear in Chapter 4. I should also like to thank the associates and staff whom I have had the good fortune of meeting and working with at the Center for Religious Development in Cambridge over a number of years for their questions, honesty, sensitivity, patience, and friendship. Of course in the matter of spiritual direction we learn far more from being with people than we do from reading books, the present work included. Direction is more a matter of practice than of theory. Still, books—even small ones—have their place. To all my anonymous teachers, especially the little ones, I say thanks.

Casa Santa María del Camino
The Second Week of Lent, 2003

Introduction

Spiritual direction can certainly be described as practical in nature, but behind the practice there lies a theory—or better, a theology. To take a parallel example, consider liturgical practice. Behind the practice, action, or performance of ritual and sacrament there lies theory: a theology of the Church and of grace, a theology of revelation and redemption, a theology of sacrament and of mission, even a theology of the body. Neither the presider nor the members of the assembly may be explicitly aware of the many theological determinants of the community's actions and words while they are engaged in a liturgical celebration, but those determinants are operative nonetheless. So also with spiritual direction. Neither individual directors nor those they direct may be conscious of the theology that underpins its practice, but Christian spiritual direction rests on foundations.

Those who have had the opportunity either to give or to receive spiritual direction can readily attest to its benefits: people really do learn to become more God-centered and grow in their awareness of the divine presence that constantly surrounds them. Some Christians have dedicated themselves to full-time work in the ministry of spiritual direction, others part-time. Some have spiritual directors whom they speak with on a regular basis; others seek a spiritual director only from time to time. The vast majority of Christians have most likely never been involved in the giving or receiving of spiritual direction in any formal sense. Once the nature of spiritual direction has been explained to them, however, and once they see its place within the overall functioning and wellbeing of Christian communities, the reality of spiritual direction may seem far less remote or esoteric. Spiritual direction occurs on a regular, maybe even on a daily basis in numerous informal ways. Even those living at the fringe of institutional religion may have recourse to spiritual direction, as Tilden Edwards writes: "Spiritual direction already serves as a kind of 'halfway house' for a number of unchurched people who believe in God and are serious about their spiritual lives, but for various reasons cannot at the moment commit themselves fully to a formal Christian community."[1]

My concern in these pages is not how one goes about giving direction, nor is it my aim—at least not directly—to offer spiritual guidance to those looking to strengthen or improve their relationship with God. Many manuals and books are already available on these topics. Suffice it to say that the primary requirement for someone who wants to assist others by being a spiritual director—besides being a person who lives from faith[2]—is that she or he be an attentive, discerning listener. And the primary disposition of someone looking for direction is not docility or obedience, but the ability to notice and speak honestly about what has been happening in his or her life. Everything else that takes place in the practice of direction builds on these acts of listening and noticing.

This book, then, is about what the practice of spiritual direction presupposes, and first and foremost spiritual direction rests upon a theology of revelation. I do not mean to imply that it rests upon an abstraction— "the theology of . . . ." Direction presumes that God continues to communicate the divine presence and life to human beings who are constantly being formed or created in ways not significantly different from the classic accounts of God's speaking to women and men that we find in Scripture. Our encounters with God are not occasioned by burning bushes, other-worldly visitors, or whirlwinds; the figures whose stories are told in the Bible probably did not encounter God in such supernatural ways, either. Nevertheless, revelation, when understood as God's self-communication,[3] is always happening. As Avery Dulles writes, "A comprehensive

1. Tilden Edwards, *Spiritual Direction, Spiritual Companion: Guide to Tending the Soul* (Mahwah, N.J.: Paulist Press, 2001) 186–87.

2. "Look at the proud! Their spirit is not right in them, but the righteous live by their faith" (Hab 2:4).

3. See Vatican II's Dogmatic Constitution on Divine Revelation (Dei Verbum) No. 2 and No. 6. The theological significance of these conciliar texts in which revelation is presented preeminently in personal terms has been noted frequently. Richard McBrien writes, "[Vatican II] views revelation essentially as God's self-communication, a loving and totally gratuitous invitation to enter a dialogue of friendship." See his *Catholicism*, new ed. (San Francisco: HarperSanFrancisco, 1994) 246; and the suggested readings on 272–73. And as Karl Rahner explained: "Divine self-communication means, then, that God can communicate himself in his own reality to what is not divine without ceasing to

doctrine of revelation, then, cannot limit itself to God's self-disclosure in biblical times; it must deal with God's active presence to the church and the world today, without which the good news of the gospel, which is admittedly normative, might easily be dismissed as a piece of inconsequential historical information."[4] Vatican II was able to clarify or articulate the personal dimension of revelation for the very important reason that believers over centuries have repeatedly experienced God's entrance into their lives and have known God to be part of their individual histories. At the risk of oversimplifying the revelatory process, I want to say simply that the divine mystery is first experienced and only afterwards is it schematized or analyzed in terms of a "theology of." The so-called "structure of revelation" is nothing more than a description of what happens when human beings discover God.[5]

Although the word "experience" sounds straightforward and concrete, it is actually a lot more complex than first appears. In order to avoid reducing experience to meaning raw sense data, it is important for us to understand that experience is necessarily connected to the mind's activity of interpreting what comes to us through sense and memory. Experience, furthermore, is never very far from the activity of our imaginations. The prominence of the word "experience" in contemporary theology and the ministry of spiritual direction derives from an understanding of how the mind works—how it achieves insight and how knowledge becomes personal. While doctrine and creed play a vital role in the life of faith, unless we make our own the truths that we profess, our faith will remain detached from our hearts. Doctrine—the truths we profess—arises from the Christian community's encounter with the mystery of God. And that encounter,

be infinite reality and absolute mystery, and without man ceasing to be a finite existent different from God." See *Foundations of Christian Faith: An Introduction to the Idea of Christianity*, trans. William Dych (New York: The Seabury Press, 1978) 119.

4. Avery Dulles, "Faith and Revelation," in Francis Schüssler Fiorenza and John P. Galvin, eds., *Systematic Theology: Roman Catholic Perspectives* (Minneapolis: Fortress Press, 1991) 103. By the same token, the one who reads the Gospels must be as inspired as the evangelists who composed them if the believer is to discover there the real presence of Christ.

5. See Roger Haight, *Dynamics of Theology* (Maryknoll, N.Y.: Orbis Books, 2001; first published 1990) 51–67. The challenge in working out a theory of revelation is not to lose sight of the specific religious experience on the basis of which reflection begins. Religion is interesting, not because of the generalizations we make about the religious dimension of human life, but because of the astonishing particularity of God's self-disclosure to individuals and communities. Thus we have the terms "general revelation" and "special revelation."

mediated through the Christian story, liturgical celebration, and ascetical and moral practice, is repeatable across generations. If we never really meet and know God, our doctrines, rituals, and practices are bound to remain lifeless. In short, attending to experience is central to the effectiveness of spiritual direction because enduring knowledge of God emerges "from below," that is, from within the human world, from within human history, and from the ordinariness of everyday life.[6]

Second, spiritual direction rests upon a theology of the Church. The Church, like the process of revelation, is not an abstraction but a reality that we experience, a reality that flows into and further shapes who and what we are. Church, like revelation, "happens"; both are what might be called "Spirit events." Ideas are real, too, but not all ideas are concretized through actions and relationships. We know what the Church is insofar as we experience ourselves called by the Spirit to live in and for the Lord Jesus, not just individually but together. Direction assumes the practice and interpersonal dynamics of believers coming together. They sense themselves joined at a level and in a manner that can be described, but the communion they describe cannot be adequately understood without participating in it. In other words, spiritual direction presumes the existence of Christian communities, even when the person seeking direction comes from the margins of ecclesial life.

A person cannot claim to be Christian and pretend to have no connection with or dependence upon those who have followed Jesus before us. Thus the director obviously stands within a tradition of belief and practice. It can safely be stated that the Spirit of Jesus characteristically draws believers together into a communion of life, practice, and worship. The gospel preached, prayed upon, and practiced orients people toward a joint listening to the word of God.[7] Insofar as it is rooted in the gospel, therefore, the process of spiritual direction presupposes the graced movement of the individual to an ever fuller and more visible sharing of our common life. I am not saying that men and women at the religious margins will consequently start attending church regularly. There are, after all, Christian solitaries and the existence of such men and women reminds us that

6. See the entry under "Experience" by Tad Dunne in *The New Dictionary of Catholic Spirituality*, ed. Michael Downey (Collegeville, Minn.: The Liturgical Press, 1993) 365–77. Also, George Schner, S.J., "The Appeal to Experience," *Theological Studies* 53:1 (1992) 40–59. For an interesting case study, see Kilian McDonnell, O.S.B., "Spirit and Experience in Bernard of Clairvaux," *Theological Studies* 58:1 (1997) 3–18.
7. See Mark 3:32-35.

some Christian lives follow unconventional paths to God. I am convinced, however, that God relates to us as a race. While God loves us personally and knows us each by name, as daughters and sons, God also beholds us from the perspective of our final destiny—a communion of life and love with one another which will be inseparable from our union with the holy mystery that created us. Church is a precursor of what awaits us; the virtues of compassion and solidarity in this life are absolutely integral to the Christian experience God.

Spiritual direction presupposes, thirdly, that the one giving direction has grasped in its totality the sacred narrative of Christian faith that comes to us in the Gospels. I do not mean that directors need to be skilled exegetes or systematic theologians. But they need to know what the story of Jesus is—and is not—about. There are, after all, versions of the Christian story that have impeded the development of adult relationships with God. Yet directors who suspend or bracket their doctrinal prejudices—or beliefs—are not necessarily better listeners on that account. All of us hear and interpret what others share with us through our own categories; that much is an inescapable condition of our humanness. We need to be as aware as possible, therefore, of what those filters or categories are, where they came from, and how they affect the way we read and interpret other people's lives. A Christian spiritual director does not "operate" from a religiously neutral position when it comes to observing the presence and action of God in human life and history, but from a particular configuration of faith (there are, after all, other religions and thus other ways for faith in God to be configured) and from an imagination trained by the story of Jesus. This is a major point and one that will occupy us considerably in the pages that follow. The enduring strength of the Christian religion comes from the gospel narrative—and its enduring weakness comes from the fact that far too often the gospel story stops growing within us as the years pass because, some say, it is "only" a story.

Fourth, the practice of spiritual direction presupposes an understanding of what it means to be human. This point is so obvious that it hardly seems necessary to state it, but for the sake of completeness it ought to be mentioned. In technical terms an understanding of what it is to be human would be called a "theological anthropology"—a handy expression for theologians but one that conveys very little to a nonspecialist. We come from God. We live, move, and have our being in God. God is our final destiny. These three assertions frame in a nutshell an authentically Christian philosophy of life. The wound within human thinking and choosing that we refer to as original sin; the mystery of divine love as the ultimate reason why we exist at all; the human being as constituted in such a way that the mystery of God is woven into the way our minds and hearts function; the eschatological pull upon the human heart that prevents us from making humanity the measure of all things: these ideas become the master strokes by which our nature has been brushed and shaded. For a spiritual director, they are requisite habits of the mind. For the one seeking direction, these habits initially might be rather undeveloped. Spiritual literacy—a felt familiarity with basic Christian convictions about the human being in its relation to God—should not be presumed.

One other point should be added here. The human "self" is essentially social in nature. I do not mean simply that God intends our existence to be communitarian; I take for granted that solidarity is a virtue to be vigorously cultivated. In saying that the self is essentially social I mean that we do not exist as individual islands of consciousness, but from the moment of conception we exist in relation to other selves. What we become is in large measure determined by what others do (or fail to do) with their freedom. Not exclusively, of course; life gives us room to take many initiatives for ourselves. But we do not merely exist and grow alongside each other; we penetrate one another's space and our being gets woven into theirs, and vice versa. The importance of this fact has to be emphasized precisely because today in North Atlantic culture, as Rowan Williams puts it, stress upon the individual has obscured the social nature of the human self and led to a "loss of soul."[8] We make important choices, for example, often without attending to their consequences within the various circles to which we belong—families, civic community, the assembly of believers, and (however unconnected to us they may seem) the other human beings who inhabit this planet. And because spiritual direction attends so closely to the individual's relationship with God, care must exercised so that direction does not unwittingly play into the age's preoccupation with the private, individualized self making its mark upon the world. The social self is primed to become an "ecclesial self."[9]

8. Rowan Williams, *Lost Icons: Reflections on Cultural Bereavement* (Harrisburg, Penn.: Morehouse Publishing Co., 2000).
9. See Stanley J. Grenz, *The Social God and the Relational Self: A Trinitarian Theology of the Imago Dei* (Louisville, Ky.: Westminster John Knox Press, 2001) 312ff.

I first started to think about the suppositions underlying spiritual direction after a number of discussions about whether and under what conditions it would be possible for a Christian to be a spiritual director for a person who is not Christian. For over fifteen years I had been giving a series of presentations to associates at the Center for Religious Development in Cambridge, Massachusetts, in a program preparing them for the ministry of spiritual direction, or if they were already directing others, helping them to carry on that ministry more effectively.[10] Initially my assignment was to conduct a seminar on the relation between theology and experience. The purpose of the seminar was to look at the legitimacy of experience, which is often juxtaposed with doctrine, in the craft of thinking theologically and to appreciate the priority of experience over its conceptualization which theology as a whole represents.

Religious literacy, I had concluded some years ago, has two aspects. A balanced faith life requires both doctrinal literacy, which many of us acquire fairly early in life, and spiritual literacy, which frequently remains either infantile or woefully unconnected with doctrines and creeds well into adulthood.[11] Many of us acquire early in life a rudimentary familiarity with the core Christian beliefs, at least enough to give them lip service when we recite the Creed during Mass. As youngsters our sense of God may have been real and nourishing, but for the most part it lacked integration with doctrine and creed. Spiritual direction is therefore an important resource for Christian communities at the moment when people begin looking for greater depth and clarity in their relationship with God. But this relationship will lose its Christian distinctiveness to the degree that we do not understand the Church's sacred narratives or the symbolic structure of our religious assertions. If the Church's ministers could ever step back and listen to what goes on all over the world as women and men engage in spiritual direction, the resulting insight would, I suspect, take their collective theological breath away. For the more men and women attend to their experience of God, the more the rest of us would hear what in Christian faith really counts, which beliefs are appropriated or internalized and which ones are left aside, and how variegated is the human

---

10. For history and background on the Center, see Madeline Birmingham and William J. Connolly, *Witnessing to the Fire: Spiritual Direction and the Development of Directors, One Center's Experience* (Kansas City, Mo.: Sheed & Ward, 1994).

11. See W. Reiser, "Spiritual Literacy: Some Basic Elements," *Lumen Vitae* 42:3 (1987) 329–48.

relationship with the divine mystery. There, in the process of direction, the core beliefs about the divine mystery itself are shown to be confirmed or disconfirmed: that God is good, that God is personal, that God is love, or that God is compassionate. Whenever assertions such as these come alive—that is, whenever they start to inform and shape everyday human existence—then they can properly be called truths and not merely theologically correct propositions.[12]

In addition to assisting believers discern the will of God in their lives, the process of direction enables people to achieve balance between mind and heart, and integration of narrative, symbol, and personal experience. In short, the spiritual director cannot be indifferent to the quality of an individual's doctrinal literacy. Although a spiritual director qua director is not a catechist, a theologian, an apologist, or a professional teacher, his or her effectiveness can be limited by the directee's unfamiliarity with the basics of Christian faith, assuming for the time being that the person belongs to the Christian tradition. Ignatius Loyola realized that not everyone was equally suited to making the Spiritual Exercises in their entirety; thus the Exercises would need to be adapted to a person's "age, education, and ability." Some people who want to make the Exercises may be "uneducated," "simple," "illiterate," "poorly qualified," or possess "little natural capacity."[13] The director does not interrupt the process at that point and offer an abbreviated course in religion, but the desire to know God more intimately may sometimes have to be put on hold because holy desires are impeded by religious illiteracy. Those familiar with the Autobiography or Reminiscences of St. Ignatius will recall how he described God's acting in his life as a teacher with a schoolboy, for after his conversion Ignatius was realizing how rudimentary his understanding of spiritual matters was.[14] With good reason, then, does the gospel portray Jesus as a teacher. The disciples were slow learners—hardhearted, deaf, blind, chronically incapable of grasping the divine "logic"—and thus they needed a patient instructor. At the out-

---

12. I have spelled this out in more detail in *The Potter's Touch: God Calls Us to Life* (Mahwah, N.J.: Paulist Press, 1981) 17–49; and "Truth and Life," *The Way* 19:4 (1979) 251–60.

13. See the Eighteenth Annotation to the Spiritual Exercises.

14. "God treated him at this time just as a schoolmaster treats a child whom he is teaching. Whether this was because of his lack of education and of brains, or because he had no one to teach him, or because of the strong desire God himself had given him to serve him, he believed without doubt and has always believed that God treated him this way." See *Ignatius of Loyola: The Spiritual Exercises and Selected Works*, ed. George E. Ganss (Mahwah, N.J.: Paulist Press, 1991) 79.

set those whom Jesus called were not all that literate, religiously speaking—at least according to their gospel portraits. It's not that they did not know the doctrines or teachings of their faith but that they had a great deal more to learn about the mystery of God.

In actuality, the relation between experience and concepts or ideas is far more complex than meets the eye. "Pure" experience does not exist, except, as we noted a moment ago, in the case of raw sense data. The mind—ears, eyes, and brain—are forever interpreting the world and even the non-public events which happen inside of us. Becoming aware of what determines precisely how and why we interpret the world the way we do involves a lengthy process of self-discovery.

At any rate, as the years went by I noticed that the associates had pretty much covered the more obvious issues connected with experience before arriving at the Center. They had been reading solid works of contemporary theology and biblical study, and theologians today take pretty much for granted what an older generation had to defend vigorously in the wake of the Modernist crisis and the magisterium's suspicion of appeals to experience. Ignatius Loyola, I might point out, had defended himself against a similar suspicion about religious experience because of his conviction that during the course of the Spiritual Exercises God communicates directly with the believer. But if God meets us so immediately in the inwardness of our hearts and minds, then God must also be there to meet us in daily life, the arena in which the will of God unfolds and faith proves itself by deeds.[15]

Instead of continuing in my course to concentrate on the role of experience in theological reflection, therefore, I went on to pay more attention to the Jesus story itself, together with the religious experience of Jesus and the early communities as it is refracted through the writings of the New Testament. I made this change for several reasons. In the same way that experience had emerged and established itself as a major theological category, research into the human, historical Jesus was having its own ripple effect upon theological reflection in the Church. The more we were learning about Jesus of Nazareth—seeing Jesus in the fuller context of his own time and place, his own social and historical setting, and appreciating

---

15. Ignatius was suspected by various inquisitors of being one of the "Alumbrados" or Illuminati. See Hugo Rahner, *Ignatius the Theologian,* trans. Michael Barry (New York: Herder and Herder, 1968) 156–65. See also my Foreword to *The Spiritual Exercises of Saint Ignatius,* trans. Pierre Wolff (Liguori, Mo.: Triumph, 1997) xiii–xvii.

Jesus as "truly human," as fully one of us, with his own religious and cultural "experience"—the more we had to adjust our thinking about many other elements of belief. The way we viewed God, the Church, revelation, sacraments, redemption, eschatology, even history and human nature itself—all of our major religious points needed to be revisited in light of our growing understanding of the foundational writings that comprise the New Testament.

From thinking about Jesus' experience, it was but a short step to wonder in what way his experience of God and the world might be normative for his followers.[16] Or to put the point in terms of a question: Can a Christian today appropriate the gospel story without appropriating the underlying religious experience that got the story going in the first place? Can one know Jesus without sharing his experience of God? Knowing Jesus and knowing about Jesus are two different things. All the scholarly information in the world about Jesus does not translate into having a faith-relationship with him. At the same time, however, I would argue that a faith-relationship can never prescind entirely from a scholarly retrieval of the historical Jesus. And central to that retrieval would be the faith or religious experience of Jesus himself—a faith that will always remain indelibly Jewish, for the interior life of Jesus would be incomprehensible apart from the religious history of his people.

Direction and the religious situation today

There is a heightened yet healthy awareness today of other religious traditions and all of us stand to learn a lot from them. I would even suggest that just as Catholic theology cannot be undertaken without a thorough grounding in Scripture, so also what we think God is like and thus how we relate to God in prayer should not unfold in a religious or cultural vacuum. Theology today has to be done "comparatively," that is, with one eye on what others have to share with us about their experience of God. But we shall be in a position to draw fruit from other religious traditions in proportion to how much we have appropriated our own Christian

---

16. Speaking about Jesus' religious experience should not be confused with fruitless efforts to get inside his psyche. We can presume, for example, that Jesus prayed the psalms and thus would have shared some of the basic human sentiments that gave rise to those prayers. In some measure we can extrapolate from his teaching and actions the faith that stands beneath them. But that is about as far as we can go. See N. T. Wright, *Jesus and the Victory of God* (Minneapolis, Minn.: Fortress Press, 1996) 479f.

faith. The point at which the spiritual traditions of the world intimidate us or tempt us to raise the volume of our religious declarations is the moment in which we need to undertake an inventory of our insecurities.

Christians have apprenticed themselves to non-Christians known for their learning and holiness, and non-Christians have approached Christians looking for inner peace, guidance, and compassionate listening. Perhaps the simple fact that we are human is enough to link us on a common quest for the divine mystery. Some of the insights gained from engaging in that quest thus belong to the spiritual patrimony of the human race. All over the world Christians have established houses of prayer and retreat centers, many of which are in lands where Christianity is a minority religion. Yet the spiritual tone of those centers and houses is often remarkably edifying for its honesty and its humility. "This is how the divine mystery has revealed itself to us," they say; "how has it been revealed to you?"

But a person's religious tradition is hardly a disposable shell enclosing a universal spiritual experience. Just how much is a Christian spiritual director really capable of hearing or attending to what a non-Christian says? One obviously listens to the words, the narrative history; but does one hear the culture, the religious and philosophical assumptions about life, and so forth? In order to answer this, of course, the Church is going to have to turn to the experience of those who have engaged in interreligious dialogue and have faced head-on the tension between the universal and the particular elements of Christian faith and practice.[17]

The question may not strike the reader as all that pressing, especially if this sort of situation arises only infrequently because one is not living at the ecumenical edge of modern life. The advantage of the question, however, is that it forces us to reflect on what the practice of spiritual direction assumes. I shall attempt to argue that a Christian spiritual director, while helping another to recognize the action of God in his or her life, is not merely an astute though neutral observer. Rather, the director as a person steeped in the Christian experience of God becomes an advocate of the

---

17. For instance, Francis X. Clooney, "A Charism for Dialog: Advice from the Early Jesuit Missionaries in Our World of Religious Pluralism," *Studies in the Spirituality of Jesuits* 34:2 (2002). In this regard Thomas Merton, with his vocational interest in monasticism and the world religions, is a parable for the present ecclesial moment—I mean the Merton of *Zen and the Birds of Appetite, The Way of Chuang Tzu, Mystics and Zen Masters*, or *The Asian Journal*. Also, see Peter C. Phan, "Multiple Religious Belonging: Opportunities and Challenges for Theology and Church," *Theological Studies* 64:3 (2003) 495–519. The notion of "multiple religious belonging" is theologically intriguing and,

Gospel by the sheer fact of being there for the other, even though the director may not consider herself or himself to be engaged in any sort of "missionary" or catechetical activity.

I agree with those who have studied comparative mysticisms that there is a connection between the Christian mystical experience and the deep religious experience of, say, Buddhist or Muslim mystics. It strikes me, however, that the mysticism in question is associated primarily with the apophatic tradition and that apophatic mysticism, with its stress upon the experience of not-knowing, belongs to the religious heritage of the human race.[18] To put the matter a bit differently, Jesus did not invent religion and thus Christians have no biblical warrant to preempt the religious potential of the human race. Our claims about God must always be governed by modesty. Language, just like one's cultural place and historical moment, has its obvious limitations. Yet far more importantly human beings find themselves at the mercy of a light that absolutely transcends us, even to the point of blinding our most ambitious efforts to grasp what God is like.

But there is another type of mysticism represented by the kataphatic tradition. This tradition, which emphasizes what can be said "positively" about God on the basis of Scripture and salvation history, takes as its starting point the existence of religious particularity. Jesus is not (and can never be) Moses, the Buddha, the Prophet—or any other religious figure. Whatever similarities people may discern between his teaching and that of other figures renowned for holiness, Jesus is irreversibly defined by the social, cultural, and historical situation in which he lived. The mystery to be discovered in the case of Jesus, or in the case of any human being, is the mystery of irreducible difference. Each and every human being has a relationship with God that is both special and distinctive; each one of us is different—the very hairs of our head are numbered and known to God.

---

from the viewpoint of spiritual direction, potentially quite challenging. But the idea that "revelation and salvation, brought by Jesus, is somehow present in other religious traditions" (509) slides too quickly, I think, over the narrative lines that determine the distinctiveness of the Christian experience of salvation.

18. The apophatic moment is important for the vibrancy and health of theology and not just for spirituality, because in that moment theology itself gets cleansed of any pretense. Theologians are then forced to say, "I don't know." Yet the fact or occurrence of revelatory experience draws attention to the insufficiency of the apophatic moment. Because they are believers, theologians, like spiritual directors and everyone else, must be able to say, "I have met and I do know God." The God who is absolute mystery is at the same time, with a bow to Arundhati Roy, the God of small things.

But neither can Jesus' "difference" simply be set alongside everyone else's, for reasons that all of us comprehend almost instinctively.

I hope that what follows will be helpful to those engaged in the practice of spiritual direction, perhaps in the way that knowledge of an automobile's engine can prove useful to people who drive. I, for one, am at the mercy of mechanics; but why stop there? I am at the mercy of specialists of all sorts; so are we all. Yet while I flush a toilet without knowing how to install one, use a computer without knowing how to build one, or can learn to read a Vedic text without knowing how to translate Sanskrit, I know how reassuring and satisfying it would be to possess those skills.[19] In the business of looking for God, however, we don't have the luxury of entrusting ourselves to the experts. Nobody can make the journey of faith in our stead. We turn to others for guidance and wisdom, but each has to walk the path for herself or himself and take responsibility for the journey's outcome. I am hoping, then, that this book will be helpful to some other travelers along the way.

19. We all have emotions and feelings, too, although few of us understand their biochemistry and the brain function that makes feelings possible; we are not neurobiologists. Nevertheless, since feelings figure so prominently into the process of discernment, the more we know about what they are and how they get turned on and off, the sharper our understanding of how the Creator "works directly" *[. . . deje inmediate obrar al Criador con la criatura]* with the creature (see the Exercises, no. 15)—and the less likely we will be to mystify their genesis. To state the obvious, feelings can be key indicators of how and where we perceive the presence or absence of God if (and only if) the mystery of God has been acknowledged and welcomed as the centering reality of our life. In other words, feelings alone would probably not bring human beings to God. Some message, story, or wisdom needs to be preached; the word "God" has to be heard. For a scientific examination of feeling see Antonio Damasio, *Looking for Spinoza: Joy, Sorrow, and the Feeling Brain* (Orlando, Fl.: Harcourt, Inc., 2002) 3–179. Damasio writes: "Yet, spiritual experiences, religious or otherwise, are mental processes. They are biological processes of the highest level of complexity. They occur in the brain of a given organism in certain circumstances and there is no reason why we should shy away from describing those processes in neurobiological terms provided we are aware of the limitations of the exercise. . . . Accounting for the physiological process behind the spiritual does not explain the mystery of the life process to which that particular feeling is connected. It reveals the connection to the mystery but not the mystery itself" (284, 286–87).

Chapter 1

It Is God Who Reveals:
Direction and Revelation

No attentive spiritual director would be unfamiliar with the stunning diversity and intricacy in the way human beings search for God. While understandably drawing upon insights gained as their own interior lives have developed, directors learn early that they cannot map in advance how another Christian's journey will unfold or what that person's growth in God is going to look like. Not only can individual details vary considerably, but one cannot predict with absolute certainty that each Christian's journey or "progress" will eventually conform to an overall pattern of the interior life.

Many people, in my experience, tend to think of their religious lives as fairly conventional and unremarkable. They practice their faith in the modest, customary ways of formal worship, private prayer, and traditional moral practice based on the Ten Commandments and the twofold command to love God above all things and their neighbor as themselves; it would never occur to them that they have had visionary moments or mystical experiences. If asked whether they knew God or had experienced God, they would probably answer no or that they were unsure. If asked whether they believed in God and prayed to God, they would answer a confident yes.

Some diversity with respect to how we lead our lives as believers is to be expected, of course. The dominant patterns of Christian living—marriage, orders, and religious life—have their distinctive sacramental or, in the case of religious life, quasi-sacramental expressions and corresponding spiritualities. For a long time we have tended to bounce our spiritual identities against those recognized vocational classifications. Until now at least, the three traditional forms or "states of life" have broadly determined how we position ourselves in the Church and how we evaluate our Christian practice, although I should point out that the classical "states" do not exhaust all the evangelical possibilities. One can choose to be single in the world, devout and Gospel-minded though unaffiliated with any religious community. There are inner-city hermits, there are people whom I would characterize as habitual pilgrims, there are ordinary people who share life under the same roof as "friends in the Lord," and there are Catholic Worker houses, L'Arche communities, and ashrams. What joins these forms or patterns of Christian existence together is baptism, as we read in Ephesians: "There is one body and one Spirit, just as you were called to the one hope of your calling, one Lord, one faith, one baptism, one God and Father of all, who is above all and through all and in all" (Eph 4:4-6).

This claim to spiritual oneness grounded in baptism is a bit deceptive, however. During Sunday parish liturgies, for example, we behold a single assembly gathered for worship: all signing themselves with the cross, all listening to the same readings and professing the same creed, all sharing the one bread and cup. Yet if someone with keen interviewing skills were to get these same folks talking about the shape and direction of their lives, I suspect it would be discovered in short order that, when examined from underneath, the gestures and actions which make us appear and sound religiously so much alike conform only slightly to what has been going on inside. Indeed, classifying people according to states of life or forms of Christian existence can be just as misleading. The outward form or state may be the same, whether we are married, evangelically single, religious, or ordained, but one's outward observance or pattern of life is seldom an adequate let alone complete expression of inner reality. Once we move beyond the customary markers of religious practice the distinctive way our relationship with God has developed is likely to surprise us. In many respects, when it comes to looking for God we behave more like hikers leaving the beaten path to discover the countryside on their own than like marching bands or people in a Corpus Christi procession.

Many Christian Paths

There is a wild unpredictability to the way of the Spirit. I do not mean that no two paths to God are identical, which may or may not be true, depending on how one defines "path." Peter and John, for instance, were destined to follow Jesus in different directions, one having his belt fastened and led where he would not want to go, and the other remaining until Jesus came; yet both had "followed."[1] The major religions of the world are often referred to as "ways" or "paths." Christians walk one path, Hindus another, Muslims still another, and so on—many believers treading the spiritual "path" of their tradition. What I do mean is that each person's way to God is in many respects unique. A monk once replied to a woman seeking advice about which spiritual path she ought to take by indicating a field blanketed with snow. Just follow the path, he said, to the other side. Seeing no footsteps in the snow she asked where the path was. "Exactly," he answered. "You have to create your own!"[2]

Personal landscapes are capable of endless, subtle variations. Geography, historical moment, culture, language, social and economic class—these are among the broad determinants of each person's biography. But equally significant are the numerous local elements that contribute to how we have been formed and nurtured—our genetic past, the behavior of our parents, other individuals whose lives immediately impact our own, schools, favorite authors, and so on. A naturalist with an eye for spiritual diversity and randomness would have a field day with any one of us! The potential exists, therefore, for the grace of God to be diffracted within the human world in far more ways than we could ever measure or count.

Nevertheless, in claiming that the Spirit's way is unpredictable I do not mean to call attention, simply, to the infinite details that make us so splendidly diverse. Instead I want to underline the absolute sovereignty of the Spirit in everything that touches upon our interior lives. The Spirit normally draws us gradually, almost imperceptibly into a deeper life with God and one another, as in the parable of the wheat that grows slowly, quietly, surely.[3] Yet neither is it by any means uncharacteristic of the Spirit to shake and even turn upside down the intuitions upon which we have built our lives. The same Spirit that descends upon our hearts with the

1. John 21:15-23.
2. Memory tells me that the monk was Thomas Merton but I have been unable to recall where I came across the incident. Margaret Silf attends to multiple paths in *Wayfaring: A Gospel Journey into Life* (New York: Doubleday, 2001).
3. Mark 4:26-29.

graceful movement of a dove can drive us into life's sultry wastelands where no one gets out without being tested and scarred.

In some cases, the Spirit may impel people to put aside one set of commitments in favor of another, as when Saul the Pharisee became Paul the apostle or when John Henry Newman left the Anglican Church and joined the Church of Rome or when Agnes Gonxha Bojaxhiu left the Sisters of Loreto and later as Mother Teresa founded the Missionaries of Charity or when Oscar Romero parted ways with the El Salvadoran aristocracy and found himself aligned with embattled campesinos. The sovereignty of the Spirit is also evident in the parable where the younger son had to leave home and behold the world from far beyond his father's house before he could appreciate how richly blessed he had been, for God was no less present at the beginning than at the end of the story. The father, after all, watched him leave, and the father was there to greet the boy when he found his way back.[4]

Most of us would probably be reluctant to admit that an individual who leaves the Catholic Church to join, say, the Society of Friends or the Jewish faith or Buddhism or Islam might be following the Spirit's lead. After all, is not the Spirit supposed to be the Spirit of Jesus? Nevertheless, it must be said that whenever individuals embark upon a search for God, making that search the central business of their lives, they must be responding to an overture of grace. Wherever the search takes them, there they must go, however disconcerting the process may occasionally be for the rest of us. The God of holy endings is at the same time the mystery behind awkward, even flawed beginnings. While it is certainly God's will that all share the divine life, it is hardly self-evident that God has willed that all should first know Christ.[5]

---

4. Luke 15:20.

5. The Declaration on Religious Freedom (*Dignitatis Humanae*) of Vatican II reaffirms that the human response to God in faith has to be free and that no one must be forced into Christian belief (see No. 10). We are bound to obey our conscience but stand under no compulsion when it comes to serving God (No. 11). People might leave the Church for a variety of tragic reasons—scandal would be the gravest, as Mark 9:42 makes clear—but it is conceivable that in some instances the route to wholeness, for reasons known only to God, would take people outside the Christian community. Perhaps the only "ray of that Truth which enlightens all people" to penetrate their inner vision came from a non-Christian source (see the Declaration on Non-Christian Religions, No. 2). What this would mean in terms of a theology of salvation history goes beyond the scope of this book, but I think it has to be said that we need to work incessantly to promote vibrant communities of faith and that spiritual direction in some form should be a part of ordinary catechesis.

Yet precisely because the search for God is such a determinative under-taking, prudence suggests that we avail ourselves of whatever help we can get from one another. For although not everyone follows exactly the same path, fellow-travelers may be able to share lessons about the interior life that could make their own journeys of faith, if not less demanding, then at least a lot more secure. However solitary our own inner journey might some-times feel, the fact is that human salvation does not consist of countless in-dividual contests. We are not engaged in a private competition, each on his or her own personal playing field in the critical business of seeking and find-ing God. God creates us as a race and our nature is intrinsically relational, as the existence of friendships, marriages, families, civic communities, and the Church—the social sites where God's self-revelation ordinarily occurs—so clearly demonstrates. Mutuality is a central feature of human existence; to experience God is to live in relation. Because God created the human race, our common parentage requires that we never lose sight of the mystery which ties us together from the birth of the universe to its dissolution.[6]

As a consequence, whatever talents or abilities any of us lays claim to are in a real sense common property. These gifts include our faith, prayerful-ness, holy desires, wisdom, and all the manifestations of the Spirit's pres-ence in our lives—whatever "visions" we have received, whatever "words" God has spoken in our hearts, whatever "revelations" we may have been granted. Origen wrote, "For the end is always like the beginning."[7] Since God created the human race to be one family, then oneness is what lies ahead. The ultimate destiny of every human being is a communion with one another rooted in our union with the mystery of God, who is love. Since unity in diversity belongs to the divine intention "in the beginning" and since unity is what awaits us at the end, humanity's origin and its des-tiny have to govern how we go about making sense of divine action along

6. The already/not-yet or eschatological character of the unity God intends for the human race can be heard readily in No. 13 of The Dogmatic Constitution on the Church (*Lumen Gentium*) of Vatican II: "All human beings are called to the new people of God. Therefore this people, while re-maining one and unique, is to be spread throughout the whole world and through every age to fulfill the design of the will of God, who in the beginning made one human nature and decreed that his children who had been scattered should at last be gathered together into one (see Jn 11,52)." See Norman Tanner, ed., *Decrees of the Ecumenical Councils*, 2 vols. (Washington, D.C.: Georgetown University Press, 1990) 2:859. See also No. 1 of the Declaration on the Relation of the Church to Non-Christian Religions (*Nostra Aetate*).

7. *On First Principles*, bk. 1, chap. 6, trans. G. W. Butterworth (Gloucester, Mass.: Peter Smith, 1973) 53.

the way, throughout human history. Our theology of creation consequently furnishes criteria for discerning the action of the Spirit in history and in human life. One cannot have, in other words, a communal view of salvation and an individualistic view of revelation. This means that we need one another's help—one another's talents and gifts—along the way.

The Many Ways of Spiritual Direction

Spiritual direction takes place under many forms. The form familiar to most of us is the setting where one believer approaches another for the express purpose of talking about his or her relationship to God. In their book *The Practice of Spiritual Direction*, William Barry and William Connolly define Christian spiritual direction as "help given by one Christian to another which enables that person to pay attention to God's personal communication to him or her, to respond to this personally communicating God, to grow in intimacy with this God, and to live out the consequences of the relationship."[8] This definition echoes one of the best-known emphases of the Second Vatican Council's Dogmatic Constitution on Divine Revelation, which spoke in personal terms of the divine communication: "It has pleased God, in his goodness and wisdom, to reveal himself and to make known the secret purpose of his will (see Eph 1,9)." And again, "By divine revelation God has chosen to manifest and communicate both himself and the eternal decrees of his will for the salvation of humankind."[9] The mystery of God's will, the Constitution explains, is that human beings should have access to the Father, through Christ and in the Spirit, in order that they might share in the divine nature. Such, in a nutshell, is what salvation consists of. Since revelation happens as God's self-communication to women and men, the practice of direction becomes a permanent feature of life according to the Spirit. Direction provides the occasion for becoming more alert to the where, when, how, and why of God's presence in our lives.[10]

8. William A. Barry and William J. Connolly, *The Practice of Spiritual Direction* (New York: Seabury Press, 1982) 8.

9. Tanner, *Decrees of the Ecumenical Councils*, 2:972-73. It follows, then, that every encounter with God—every instance of divine self-communication—is at the same time a moment in the history of a person's salvation. To meet God is to be touched and further transformed by the holy mystery of God, which is love.

10. André Louf prefers the term "accompaniment," which appears to have derived from the ministry of listening to terminally ill patients: "[S]piritual accompaniment opens us to new birth. It is

Spiritual direction can also occur, albeit in a conversation that is a little less direct, when we pick up a religious book that speaks to our experience, when we read past masters of the interior life, or when we meditate on a scriptural text. In such cases, the wisdom of people who have already walked the way of faith engages our minds and imaginations. Our conversation with them through their reflections and reminiscences enables us to clarify one or another aspect of our personal experience of the divine mystery; dialogue with past masters and mistresses of the interior life challenges us to look beyond the limitations of our particular cultural and historical moment. No one age or period holds a monopoly on religious experience. The insight of our spiritual forbears facilitates our naming for today—and it must be named, however inadequately, because our awareness is directed not to an abstraction but to a You—the sacred mystery that holds every human being in a divine grasp. We in turn shall pass along whatever we have learned about God and human nature to our children and grandchildren. And their encounter with God, like ours, will be both the same and different from that of the generation which preceded them.

Spiritual direction might take place in a group setting or as one-on-one. It can be formal or informal. At times we approach someone for the express purpose of seeking direction, yet more often we may find ourselves just talking informally with others, conversing easily yet sincerely about the things that matter to us as we share a meal, take a walk, or sit on a rock and ponder the sea. If in the process we become more conscious of the presence and action of God in our lives, then I believe it should be said that mutual direction has been taking place.[11] A more formally religious setting might be the Liturgy of the Word, community faith-sharing, or a prayer group.

Married couples are frequently givers of spiritual direction for one another, although spiritual direction might not be the category that springs

---

helping someone be born to himself, to his true self, beyond his wounds and resistance. The accompanist accompanies, that is, walks beside someone on the same path." See *Grace Can Do More: Spiritual Accompaniment and Spiritual Growth* (Kalamazoo, Mich.: Cistercian Publications, 2002) 43–44. I agree with Louf that "accompaniment" more faithfully conveys the experience of the process than "direction."

11. The everydayness of spiritual direction (should we speak of spiritual direction in everyday life?) ought not be overlooked. See Thomas H. Clancy, *The Conversational Word of God: A Commentary on the Doctrine of St. Ignatius of Loyola concerning Spiritual Conversation, with Four Early Jesuit Texts* (St. Louis, Mo.: The Institute of Jesuit Sources, 1978).

to mind as they share with each other what has been happening in their lives. The mutuality that characterizes Christian friendship and which is so much a part of the experience of intimacy carries over into the way we seek and find God. Friends in the Lord are constantly directing one another, whether they realize it or not. Not only do Christians pray together on the basis of a shared life in the Spirit; not only do they listen to one another and thereby help each other to pay attention to the Spirit's movements in their thoughts and feelings. Friends also teach, motivate, support, and encourage one another simply by being who and what they are. Example and witness are powerful guides whether encountered daily and immediately through close friendships or indirectly through autobiography. Friends and fellow pilgrims bring God into focus.

Sometimes "direction" connotes instruction and has practical content. The author of the book of Proverbs, for instance, offers a considerable amount of practical guidance or "direction" for right living. The Christian ascetical tradition can point to countless people, schooled in the ways of the Spirit, whom other believers have approached for religious and moral insight, and for concrete suggestions as to how they might improve their interior lives. Thus we have many well-known spiritual classics that sustained previous generations: *The Imitation of Christ* and *The Cloud of Unknowing*, Julian of Norwich's *Revelations of Divine Love*, Thérèse of Lisieux's *Story of a Soul* and Francis de Sales' *Introduction to the Devout Life*. Direction in this sense implied a consolidation of experience and reflection that others could share.

Simple, straightforward moral instruction, coupled with the elementary religious claim that God is one and is to be loved supremely, is simply not enough nourishment to satisfy the appetite of the vast majority of people whom we would describe as God-seekers. As soon as they start to pay attention to the divine mystery as they have personally experienced it, as soon as they realize that God cannot be loved in the abstract because God is not experienced in the abstract, they are going to start searching for guidance and insight. In the talk he prepared for a meeting on Asian monasticism in December 1968—the final words he would speak—Thomas Merton reflected on the role of Buddhist monastic communities:

> The essential thing for this [the attainment of transcendence and freedom], in the Buddhist tradition, is the formation of spiritual masters who can bring it out in the hearts of people who are as yet unformed. Whenever you

have somebody capable of giving some kind of direction and instruction to a small group attempting to do this thing, attempting to love and serve God and reach union with him, you are bound to have some kind of monasticism. This kind of monasticism cannot be extinguished. It is imperishable. It represents an instinct of the human heart, and it represents a charism given by God to man. It cannot be rooted out, because it does not depend on man. It does not depend on cultural factors, and it does not depend on sociological or psychological factors. It is something much deeper.[12]

Merton's point is really an ecclesiological one. Desire gives rise to seeking, and the seeking disposes minds and hearts to receive the wisdom of spiritual masters. As soon as seekers gather around the holy ones, monasticism is born as a school of the spirit. In Christian terms, the desire for God creates communities of faith—and vice versa, as we shall see. This means that it makes little religious sense to preach and to teach without at the same time creating opportunities where people can talk about their experience of God *and* learn from one another.

Before leaving this section I should like to offer two observations. First, the Great Commandment of Deuteronomy 6:4-5 should not be heard as a moral imperative, although its language sounds pretty coercive: "You *shall* love." When heard in that tone, people will interpret the Commandment to mean, simply, that there is a very demanding higher power whose precepts are to be followed absolutely. But love cannot be coerced, not even love of God; love can only be invited. Love implies relatedness, personal involvement, depth and beauty constantly being discovered. Perfect love of God is an eschatological reality—something we desire and aim for humbly and patiently.

The biblical injunction to love God with all our heart, mind, and strength, like the gospel command to imitate divine perfection and compassion,[13] is at its core an invitation to "taste and see,"[14] or to "come and see."[15] Anyone in the market for a streamlined religion, uncluttered by doctrines, symbols, and developed moral teaching, will eventually learn that there is no fast-track to union with God. For that very reason spiritual direction involves much more than communicating the content of

---

12. See *The Asian Journal of Thomas Merton*, ed. Naomi Burton, Patrick Hart, and James Laughlin (New York: New Directions, 1973) 342–43.

13. Matt 5:48; Luke 6:36.

14. Ps 34:8.

15. John 1:39.

other people's insight and experience. More than being counseled about
how to think or to act, people want to know and experience God for
themselves. Therefore the Great Commandment might more accurately
be called the Great Invitation. When one believer accompanies another in
hearing, responding to, and working out the implications of the Great Invitation, *both* are led to a fuller awareness of the divine mystery. A director
or spiritual companion is seldom merely an instrument of divine peda-
gogy, for as we watch others come to life—insofar as we listen to them
from our own desiring and seeking—the Spirit in them also fills us. How
could the deacon Philip's own faith not have been quickened, how could
the divine saving mystery not have been more fully revealed to him as he
listened to the Ethiopian official and then explained the passage from Isaiah?[16] Or even more pointedly, couldn't this have been the experience of
Jesus as he spoke to the woman of Sychar—because at the end he says, "I
have food to eat that you do not know about" (John 4:32). Whenever believers speak from their faith, the revelatory moment builds upon what
they draw from one another and give to one another. The food Jesus had
was her coming to faith, not as a prize he had won by evangelical outreach, but as confirmation of his experience that "the fields are ripe for
harvesting."

The second observation is that the Jesus of the Gospels was not a spiritual director in the way we think of the director's role today. He clearly
conversed with individuals about the reign of God, but the Gospels depict
him regularly speaking to groups: in Sabbath assemblies, in Peter's home,
before a crowd of five thousand, privately with the Twelve, and so on.
Jesus is portrayed as teacher, prophet, and savior. He is someone who
prayed and believed, and who clearly spoke to people about God. He was
almost always on the move and his ministry is better summed up in
months than in years. Thus the emergence of spiritual direction is perhaps
best understood as a paschal phenomenon; it presupposes the presence of
the risen Lord and the action of his Spirit in the community.

The Spirit Leads

Spiritual direction more broadly conceived takes into account the fact
that, no matter how much help we give each other, in the end only the

16. Acts 8:26-39.

Spirit of God truly guides or directs persons and communities. "For all who are led by the Spirit of God," Paul wrote, "are children of God" (Rom 8:14). But being "led" or "guided" refers to an attitude of mind and heart, a disposition of faith, a readiness to think the way God does and not the way human beings do.[17] Being led hardly means that the Spirit determines the practical course of action we are to take. The story in Acts about the apostles' casting lots to see who would take Judas' place, like the biblical fondness for dreams and oracles, vastly oversimplifies the Spirit's action in our midst. We do, of course, ask God's blessing upon communal deliberations. But earnest praying cannot guarantee successful outcomes and intense discernment is not a matter of second-guessing something hidden in God's mind. Besides, while the process of discernment may be fine and holy, the execution of our plans can be impeded by circumstances totally beyond our control.

Devout people are not necessarily more adept than the lukewarm at figuring out what to do in particular situations; making the "right" decision is more often than not just a combination of intelligence and luck. What believers bring to their deliberations, however, is a set of categories or values that challenge, and perhaps subvert, conventional norms of practicality, profitability, or even sometimes of propriety. Paul's declaration that what he once had prized he now counts as rubbish[18] is a perfect illustration of the surprising reversal that occurs within the Christian imagination as a result of the gospel story. The Spirit leads us not so much into making the "right" decision as putting on the mind of Christ.

Letting oneself be led or drawn by the Spirit is, of course, a central feature of the spirituality underlying the Fourth Gospel. "An intentional relationship of Christian spiritual direction," writes Carolyn Gratton, "is not so much a matter of one person having authority to direct another, rather, both parties in the relationship are expected to become attentive listeners to the Holy Spirit, who continually provides providential direction in the life of each man and woman whether they are aware of it or not."[19] And of what does this type of direction consist? Principally it consists of acquiring the faith and dispositions which were those of Jesus, of

17. Mark 8:33.
18. Phil 3:7-8.
19. Carolyn Gratton, "Spiritual Direction," in *The New Dictionary of Catholic Spirituality* (Collegeville, Minn.: The Liturgical Press, 1993) 913.

being clothed with Christ—the new nature or self of Colossians 3:10—or of being ever more deeply immersed in the mystery of his dying and rising: the New Testament knows many ways to express the same idea. Matthew, for instance, puts it this way: In whatever pertains to evangelical living, a Christian has but one teacher;[20] we should learn from him who is "gentle and humble in heart" since in his teaching we shall find freedom and rest.[21]

Not everyone consents to being drawn by the Spirit, of course. We should not presume that everybody has a spiritual life, no matter how inchoate, for there are human beings whose spirits give every indication of being either dormant or dead. Unless someone stirs or raises them, their existence will bear no lasting fruit. Some human beings, having been born into a culture of death or poverty, are truly deprived spiritually. Others, however, like the seed that fell on the footpath or among the thorns, have simply succumbed. Whatever the explanation, spiritual death is the worst affliction to which human beings are susceptible; in the deadliest scenario it creates monsters. Perhaps for this very reason, God raises up prophets, messengers, witnesses, preachers, evangelists, healers, directors of souls.

Yet whenever hearts and minds do awaken to the compassionate mystery that surrounds them, responding to that mystery becomes life's central business. However valuable and salutary another person's spiritual counsel may be as these men and women work out their response, there is no substitute for learning how to pay attention to the Spirit at work inside themselves, urging them towards deeper prayer even when they insist that they do not know how to pray[22] and filling them with holy desires.

Where, then, does the Spirit work? The Spirit's sphere of action, as it were, embraces not only a person's inner experience with its desires, fears, fantasies, consolations, and so on; it also encompasses the things we think of as external to ourselves—Scripture and sacrament, believing community and world, history, tradition and the signs of the times. The working of the Spirit does not make our sacred narratives, forms of worship, doctrines, and creeds relative; it does not reduce them to little more than cultural or anthropological instruments through which the grace of God is mediated to us. Nevertheless, the action of the Spirit cannot be curtailed

20. Matt 23:8-10.
21. Matt 11:29.
22. Rom 8:26.

or delimited by particular religious forms, either. I take this to be the point behind Jesus' exchange with the woman by Jacob's well: "Woman, believe me, the hour is coming when you will worship the Father neither on this mountain nor in Jerusalem" (John 4:21). To insist, therefore, that the Spirit is ultimately the one who directs us should not undercut the role and importance of all the externals—the creeds, rituals, narratives, symbols, art forms, inspired writings, and community prayers—that mediate our encounters with God. But at the same time, the mystery of God transcends them.

Spiritual direction appears, therefore, to involve three elements: content (instruction or counsel is communicated), practice (believers assisting one another), and attentiveness to experience. The Spirit moves from within our experience on a trajectory that reaches from the depths of a person's mind and heart to the wide horizon which is the world and human history. I want to be careful in how I state this last point. The terms "inner" and "outer" become misleading when used to describe the individual's relationship with the world. For while the self certainly resides in a zone of privacy—we speak, after all, of the "interior" life—each person's self is also socially constructed. The world, in other words, finds its way into the fibers of our imaginations, memories, desires and frustrations, feelings and moods, loyalties and fears, and so on; the world finds its way through the hundreds and thousands of "hits" it keeps making on the web page that is our souls. Thus (to take one example) Roger Haight writes:

> Paradoxically, when one tries to define the concrete human person within an historically conscious framework, the idea of a discretely autonomous individual self all but disappears. No unique individual person is merely that, because each one comes to be and develops in a network of relations that operate to define the self. Thus not only is human existence as a whole a social phenomenon, but also each human person has been socially constituted.[23]

There is far more fluidity between inner and outer than we are ordinarily conscious of. Shifting to a theological key, this means not only that the Spirit of God is far more like the air we breathe than the food we ingest,

---

23. Roger Haight, *Dynamics of Theology* (Maryknoll, N.Y.: Orbis Books, 2001; originally published 1990) 4.

but also that the Spirit is constantly prompting us to bring what is outside of us in, reminding us that we have eyes and ears precisely in order to pay attention to what is outside. The fact that each of us enjoys a "private" life which nobody else can see does not automatically imply that we also have a spiritual life. We possess the capacity for it, but I would argue that spiritual life by definition cannot develop except in relationship to the mystery of God. True, the only direction a human life ought to take is a spiritual one, although this has never meant that religiousness is a matter of being totally absorbed by ostensibly religious practices and concerns. In short, the spiritual life embraces the whole of life insofar as human beings have spirit and that spirit originates in God.

Spiritual Direction and Revelation

The theological category of revelation does not explain the divine-human encounter; it is a way of describing it. And there is no way to describe the encounter without appealing to experience. The story of Moses' first encounter with God in Exodus 3 is essentially a description of the way the God of Israel is experienced, and one does not enter into that experience without having shared first in the people's suffering. To speak about revelation, therefore, is to describe how and where we have found the mystery of God.

The difference between revelation as content and revelation as process requires little explanation. Revelation as "content" refers to what we know about God through Scripture and salvation history. But since whatever human beings know about God derives from what God has revealed to the world—"For what can be known about God is plain to them, because God has shown it to them" (Rom 1:19)—and since knowledge of God is not exclusive to the Christian faith, Christian theology further differentiates between its own "special" revelation and "general" revelation. The content of general revelation includes the fact that God has created the world and wants to save, redeem, or draw human beings to greater freedom, compassion, transcendence, unity, peace, and love. That the privileged route to all of this consists of communion with God through the risen Jesus in the Spirit would certainly constitute special revelation, according to Christian theology. Both of these forms could be developed in more detail, but the overall idea is that when many of us think of revelation, we are accustomed to think of its contents. And the religious or spiritual limitations of objectifying in this way what God "wants" us to know should be readily apparent to a spiritual director.

Because one cannot have knowledge of God unless one has also experienced God, Christian theologians have drawn attention to the fact that revelation must also be considered as a process. This process, furthermore, unfolds on various levels. The Bible itself, as a work centuries in the making, testifies to the fact that divine self-disclosure did not take place all at once in the first three chapters of Genesis. Moreover, even though Christian theology traditionally claimed that revelation concluded with the death of the last apostle, experience had taught us that the process, activity, or dynamic of God's drawing near to us both individually and as a race never came to a close. There was certainly a moment that the early Church determined to be the cut-off point after which no further writings would be classified as Scripture, thereby closing its canon of sacred writings. But that historical point was by no means the end of the Christian story, or God's redemptive outreach into human communities, or people's growth in holiness and into greater familiarity with God.

It may sound catechetically neater to maintain that divine revelation was complete with the life, death, and resurrection of Jesus because then all that remains is the need to keep on immersing ourselves in that one special and definitive revelation. It is truer to experience, however, to insist that the ongoing appropriation of the Christian mystery down through the ages is an essential consequence of God's being-with-us. We do not *feel* that revelation has finished because we *experience* ourselves to be so disconcertingly unfinished, both individually and as a race. The creation of the human being does not happen all at once and the same law applies to the communities to which we belong.

If there is any one place where the unfolding nature of revelation is confirmed, surely that place is spiritual direction. The director watches as it happens. I think it is fairly easy to understand why the revelation that occurs in a person's life takes the form of presence rather than content, of experience rather than concept, of being known rather than knowing. Encounters with God can certainly be described, although most of us would probably qualify our descriptions by insisting that words could never do full justice to the experience itself. Spiritual directors have direct and immediate evidence that human beings are encountering God in ways that are personal, historical, concrete, and redemptive. *Personal*, because there is no other way to name or characterize what we mean by "encounter." We bump into objects and stumble across new and interesting ideas. In a religious experience, however, God feels like neither an object nor an idea, but as the "other" of our lives. *Historical*, because we live, move, and perceive within the parameters of time and place. *Concrete*, because we experience nothing apart from the conditions of language and culture, image and story, materiality and bodiliness. *Redemptive*, because something always happens—whether we are conscious of it or not—whenever human beings cultivate their relationship with God. Although we use language such as "create," "forgive," "redeem," "heal," "make whole," "sanctify," "guide," or "teach" in referring to divine action, from a theological viewpoint these words simply point to modalities of a single divine action or outreach. To stand in God's presence is, practically by definition, to experience God's creative, redeeming love. On many occasions, that love can be demanding and purifying. On other occasions it is healing and unifying. On every occasion it is liberating and lifegiving. There cannot be revelation in a strictly theological sense without an experience of salvation. As with Zacchaeus, the moment at which Jesus visits our home simultaneously spells the arrival of salvation.[24]

A God Who Directs through Desire

How exactly the Spirit directs us is not so easy to account for, but it would be hard to imagine anything of a spiritual nature unfolding within a person whose heart is not set on wholeness. Every effort to clarify what we mean when we speak of the human being as spiritual seems to start with an archaeology of desire. Thus Ronald Rolheiser writes:

> Spirituality concerns what we do with desire. It takes its root in the eros inside of us and it is all about how we shape and discipline that eros. John of the Cross, the great Spanish mystic, begins his famous treatment of the soul's journey with the words: 'One dark night, fired by love's urgent longings.' For him, it is urgent longings, eros, that are the starting point of the spiritual life and, in his view, spirituality, essentially defined, is how we handle that eros.[25]

24. Luke 19:9. Here as elsewhere I am thinking of salvation as a *Christian* theological category.
25. Ronald Rolheiser, *The Holy Longing: The Search for a Christian Spirituality* (New York: Doubleday, 1999) 7.

The foundational human desire is our desire for God, since that apparently is how we have been hard-wired. In the opening paragraph of his *Confessions* Augustine gave us what might well be the best-known formulation of this elementary truth, but the theme of desire or longing frequently came up elsewhere. For instance:

> Let us return, then, to that anointing of his, let us return to that anointing that teaches within what we cannot speak; and because you cannot see now, let your role be found in longing. The whole life of a good Christian is a holy longing. But what you long for you do not yet see, but by longing you are made capacious so that when what you are to see has come, you may be filled. For just as, if you should wish to fill a pocket, and you know how big the object that will be put in is, you stretch the pocket, whether made of sackcloth or leather or any thing—you know how large a thing you will place there, and you see that the pocket is narrow. By stretching you make it more capacious. So God, by postponing, stretches the longing, by longing stretches the soul, by stretching makes it capacious. Let us long, therefore, brothers, because we are going to be filled.[26]

Now, longing for God—Augustine goes on to describe God as "the totality for which we are waiting"[27]—is not quite the same thing as the desires that become grist for the process of discernment. And not all would agree that the longing for God—"the whole life of a good Christian"—coincides neatly with a longing for heaven. The longing for God does not require that one's eyes be so set on eternity that they avoid contact with the present, but it does call for a penetrating search for the presence of God here and now. The desire for God is experienced as a desire for truth, freedom, happiness, moral integrity, communion, love, unconditional acceptance, justice—in short, a desire to be whole. So long as we have desire, we live and flourish. Since there are virtually countless things that we can crave or want—possessions, relationships, careers, momentary fancies, and so on—we learn at an early stage of our spiritual development that not all desires lead in the same direction. Desire is key, although some of the things we desire actually work against the ultimate peace and communion our hearts are looking for. Ethical teaching and moral precepts

---

26. St. Augustine, Tractate 4 on 1 John, *Tractates on the First Epistle of John*, trans. John W. Rettig, in The Fathers of the Church, vol. 92 (Washington, D.C.: Catholic University of America Press, 1995) 179.

27. Ibid., 180.

are intended therefore to steer us in the direction of a richer, holier life. They alert us to what happens when desires becomes disordered and confused and are a perpetual reminder of the mysterious origin of human freedom.[28]

God directs us, then, in the most elementary way through the unfolding of our desire for fuller life, a desire which God implanted within us when the human heart was first fashioned. But is such a view of human nature really so helpful and straightforward as it sounds? Does Augustine's memorable formulation about human restlessness take sufficiently into account the ambiguity of human desiring? Augustine knew as well as we do that the human desire for God hardly guarantees that people will actually achieve salvation. The gate, after all, is a narrow one.[29] Even if we bracket the special case of those human beings in whom the desire for God never develops, never seems to have been switched on in the first place, we are still left with a remarkable display of human religious diversity. Humankind has not yet converged on one religious form or one basic expression of their religiosity, which means that the desire for God does not lead inevitably even if asymptotically to sameness or uniformity. Not only does the world present us with a stunning array of spiritualities in the major religious traditions, but it also presents us with the virtually limitless variations upon those traditions that are to be found in individual human lives.

28. Within Buddhism, the Second Noble Truth locates desire as the cause of all suffering. So long as a trace of desire exists in us nirvana will be unattainable. For this reason Buddhism emphasizes the importance of renunciation and detachment. See Kevin Trainor, ed., *Buddhism: The Illustrated Guide* (New York: Oxford University Press, 2001) 66–67. But what about a person's "desire" for enlightenment? On this paradox, see Paul Mommaers and Jan Van Bragt, *Mysticism, Buddhist and Christian: Encounters with Jan van Ruusbroec* (New York: The Crossroad Publishing Co., 1995) 203–07. The difference between Christian and Buddhist appraisals of the role of desire in the spiritual life is thus a manifestation not only of differing ways of apprehending the world but of very different religious experiences.
29. Matt 7:13-14; Luke 13:24.

Chapter 2

Imaging Divine Action in Human Lives

Writers frequently speak about the presence or action of God in their lives with an ease and simplicity that is at once astonishing and enviable. Consider, for a moment, this excerpt from one of the letters of Thomas Merton:

> I shall cease to be a writer at least as long as I am in charge of the novices. The prospect does not trouble me. I care very little what I do now, so long as it is the will of God.
>
> Will He someday bring me after all to perfect solitude? I do not know. One thing is sure, I have made as much effort in that direction as one can make without going beyond the limits of obedience. My only task now is to remain quiet, abandoned, and in the hands of God. I have found a surprising amount of interior solitude among my novices, and even a certain exterior solitude which I had not expected. This is, after all, the quietest and most secluded corner of the monastery. So I am grateful to God for fulfilling many of my desires when seeming to deny them. I know that I am closer to Him, and that all my struggles this year formed part of His plan. I am at peace in His will.[1]

We are accustomed to encountering such candor in classics of spiritual literature such as Augustine's *Confessions* or Ignatius' *Autobiography*, yet not uncommonly in ordinary conversations (including correspondence between friends) God is mentioned with an ease and a transparency that betoken warm familiarity without a trace of pretense.[2] Whatever happens for good or for ill is viewed from the perspective of faith as part of the mysterious divine

---

1. *Survival or Prophecy?: The Letters of Thomas Merton and Jean Leclercq*, ed. Patrick Hart (New York: Farrar, Straus and Giroux, 2002) 72.

2. See also the writing of Etty Hillesum, *An Interrupted Life and Letters from Westerbork* (New York: Henry Holt, 1996); and Sojourner Truth, *The Narrative of Sojourner Truth, a Northern Slave*, in

plan that penetrates and guides our lives. That plan supposedly includes where and when we are born, who our parents are, the nature of our vocational choice, the person we marry, the schools we attend, and the friendships we establish, whether, like Merton, one gets to live in a hermitage, and so forth. Nevertheless, how much of this perspective actually derives from faith and how much of it should be attributed to pious wishing on our part requires some self-examination. Behind some of our God-talk lies the mistaken assumption that God has already worked out the basic plan for our lives and that our chief responsibility is at least to welcome that plan and, if possible, to discern it in advance.

Who of us would not welcome the assurance that we are doing exactly what is in God's mind? The trouble is, of course, that we cannot spend our entire lives trying to figure out what God wants; there would be little time left for actually doing anything constructive. One gets the impression that for some people looking for the will of God in their life is like a suspicious person attempting to decipher body language, as if every gesture, every movement of the eye, or crease of the brow harbored a secret meaning. For them, life is chock full of signs—the only thing one needs to do is learn how to interpret them.[3] The expression "It is God's will" should not be used loosely. God's will is certainly not reducible to one's lot in life, one's fate or destiny, one's physical or mental condition. Otherwise, our prevailing spiritual attitude would not be one of joy or freedom but of resignation—not the surrender of "into your hands I commend my spirit" (Luke 23:46) but resignation before what ultimately cannot be escaped.

What Does God Will?

The will of God is one of the most spiritually treacherous notions I can think of. Since seeking the divine will is often a motive that leads people

---

William L. Andrews and Henry Louis Gates, Jr., eds., *Slave Narratives* (New York: The Library of America, 2000) 567–676.

3. Thus Thomas Merton had also written: "When we speak of God's will, we are usually speaking only of some recognizable sign of His will. The signpost that points to a distant city is not the city itself, and sometimes the signs that point to a great place are in themselves insignificant and contemptible. . . . Everything that exists and everything that happens bears witness to the will of God. It is one thing to see a sign and another thing to interpret that sign correctly. . . . Of all the things and all the happenings that proclaim God's will to the world, only very few are capable of being interpreted by men. And of these few, fewer still find a capable interpreter." See *No Man Is an Island* (New York: Barnes & Noble Books, 2003; first published 1955) 61–62.

to enlist the help of a spiritual director, we need to think about what the notion of God's will means and how this notion functions in the everyday life of faith. I call it a treacherous notion, first, because individuals have not infrequently believed themselves summoned to serve the divine will by engineering unspeakable violence. Acting under the intense conviction that one is doing God's will can deafen a person to the voice of reason and prudence, and prevent the person from recognizing the presence of God in a world where weeds and wheat grow together.[4]

The notion is also treacherous for a second reason: the entanglement of divine will and human religious authority. No reasonable person questions the need for authority in the form of sacred texts, tradition, ritual, codes of behavior, models of holiness—and teachers. The problem generally arises, however, when reliance on authority circumvents the individual's need and responsibility to look for God and wait until God speaks. There is simply no mature, trustworthy alternative to experiencing God for oneself. Those charged with teaching about religion and the moral life—those upon whom communities confer authority, since from a sociological perspective authority arises "from below"—may consider themselves missioned to speak on God's behalf. But religious and moral leaders can do no more than speak from their own experience, enunciate or clarify the wisdom or lived experience of the past, or put into words what the people among whom they stand have already discovered in their own hearts and minds.

Among religious communities there is a way of thinking about obedience in which superiors are imaged to be the Lord himself speaking and directing. Paul, after all, had urged the Roman community to obey civil rulers because the authority they possess, he taught, derived from God. "Let every person be subject to the governing authorities; for there is no authority except from God, and those authorities that exist have been instituted by God. Therefore whoever resists authority resists what God has appointed" (Rom 13:1-2). The first letter of Peter states: "For the Lord's sake accept the authority of every human institution, whether of

---

4. On this score see Mark Juergensmeyer, *Terror in the Mind of God: The Global Rise of Religious Violence* (Berkeley: University of California Press, 2000). Religiously sanctioned violence—military conquest—in order to secure the land of Israel remains a deeply disturbing feature of the book of Joshua. That troubling note may have contributed to Origen's profoundly spiritual way of reading the book. See Origen, *Homilies on Joshua*, trans. Barbara J. Bruce, ed. Cynthia White, The Fathers of the Church, vol. 105 (Washington, D.C.: The Catholic University of America Press, 2002).

the emperor as supreme, or of governors, as sent by him to punish those who do wrong and to praise those who do right" (1 Peter 2:13). It is essential to bear in mind, of course, that the idea of a hierarchically structured political universe runs against all of our modern democratic tendencies; cosmology should obey politics, not the other way round. While no one advocates anarchy in the social world—and thus political and social order are essential to the common good—totalitarian or imperial regimes have lost all moral legitimacy. The legitimacy of the political order should derive from humanity itself, whose nature was created by God. One always has to evaluate power structures in terms of how they protect and promote human dignity.[5] In other words, we pray for civil leaders not because they have authority from God but because they need God's help if they are to foster and defend the common good. Neither of these New Testament texts envisions that a civil ruler ever stands in place of God.

More serious is Ephesians 6:5-7, a passage which appears in Ignatius Loyola's celebrated letter on obedience to the Jesuits of Portugal in 1553. Ignatius wrote, "Therefore I should wish that all of you would train yourselves to recognize Christ our Lord in any superior, and with all devotion reverence and obey His Divine Majesty." Ignatius then appeals to the Pauline letter: "Slaves, obey your earthly masters with fear and trembling, in singleness of heart, as you obey Christ; not only while being watched, and in order to please them, but as slaves of Christ, doing the will of God from the heart. Render service with enthusiasm, as to the Lord and not to men and women" (Eph 6:5-7). "From this you can judge," Ignatius continued, "when a religious is taken not only as superior, but expressly in the place of Christ our Lord, to serve as director and guide in the divine service, what rank he ought to hold in the mind of the inferior, and whether he ought to be looked upon as man or rather as the vicar of Christ our Lord."[6]

---

5. For instance, in their 1986 pastoral letter on the economy the U.S. bishops wrote: "Every perspective on economic life that is human, moral, and Christian must be shaped by three questions: What does the economy do *for* people? What does it do *to* people? And how do people *participate* in it?" And later: "*The dignity of the human person, realized in community with others, is the criterion against which all aspects of economic life must be measured.*" See *Economic Justice for All: Pastoral Letter on Catholic Social Teaching and the U.S. Economy* (Washington, D.C.: National Conference of Catholic Bishops, 1986) 1, 15.

6. *Letters of St. Ignatius of Loyola*, trans. William J. Young (Chicago: Loyola University Press, 1959) 288–89.

I do not think there is any doubt about what Ignatius meant: obedience is helped when the superior is regarded as representing Christ. But how far shall we press this idea—is the intention essentially christological, or is it practical and ascetical? The author of Ephesians appears to be making a practical, even a strategic point: the religious and moral superiority of the Christian community should be evident in the fact that Christian slaves are neither disobedient nor subversive—indeed, they should be even more hardworking and loyal than their non-Christian counterparts. If the managerial classes were pagan, then they would be certain to notice this moral spirit and look favorably upon the Christian movement, perhaps even to the point of joining it. Yet since the passage next includes an instruction to the masters,[7] it seems that the author is doing little more than encouraging harmony on the domestic front. What remains, then, is a rather lackluster teaching that accepts slavery as a fixture of social and economic life. Ephesians appeals to the masters to cease threatening their slaves by recalling that they serve the same Master and that in his eyes slaves and masters are equal. From a higher, religious perspective, therefore, earthly masters too should consider themselves bound to obey and serve Christ. In short, the intention of the passage seems to be a moral and practical one, its tone exhortatory. But christologically we are left with a bit of a difficulty because in the gospel narrative Jesus is portrayed more like a servant than a master; the one who is greatest becomes the servant of all.[8] Exhorting someone to obedience is one thing. Doing so by identifying the superior or master with Jesus is quite another.

In any case, the notion of obedience to Jesus is somewhat muddled. As his disciples we do, of course, try to follow his teaching. But while following may be viewed as a form of obedience, we generally do not think of ourselves as obeying an instructor just because we subscribe to his or her teaching. Rather we are entrusting ourselves to the wisdom of the teaching itself, either because we have experienced the teaching to be liberating or because out of affection for the teacher we trust the promise of new and richer life inherent in his or her words.

The fact is that Jesus does not confide to us what vocational choices we should be making or how we ought to decide critical issues in our lives, and he is not pulling tiny strings that guide the control signals which determine

7. Eph 6:9.
8. Mark 9:35; 10:45; John 13:12-15.

whether our ways will be rough or smooth. Discernment is our responsibility, and in the end no one guarantees the infallibility of what we decide. So what would it mean to obey Jesus? The best answer I can think of is that obedience consists of working steadily for the interior freedom that enables us to follow the Spirit's lead. And if that is the case, then Ignatius' proposal about imagining a superior as Christ's vicar or representative falls apart. Jesus does not give us concrete directives about what we are to do or how we are to proceed from one day to the next. Discerning what is required of us is truly a labor of faith. To draw again from Merton:

> Of one thing I am certain.
>
> My life must have meaning. This meaning springs from a creative and intelligent harmony between my will and the will of God—a clarification by right action.
>
> But what is right action? What is the will of God?
>
> What are the sources of all my confusion on these?
>
> I can no longer accept the superficial verbalism (going in circles) which evades reality by simply saying the will of the Superior is the will of God and the will of God is the will of the Superior. I do not mean that the will of the Superior does not, or cannot, indicate where God's will may be for me—but the will of the Superior simply defines and points out the way which I am to try to act intelligently and spiritually, and thus clarify the meaning of my own life ("giving glory to God").
>
> Simply to go ahead blindly, muttering "the will of God, the will of God" clarifies nothing and it is making me mentally ill. Not because obedience is unhealthy—on the contrary! But our obedience *here,* or at least mine, is unhealthy because in the first place it is not real obedience. Whose fault? We are *all* to blame. For me to say I alone am to blame would be another lie. Too many lies already!
>
> But "obedience" here tends to sanctify various lies like this one.
>
> The sanctification of falsity by the magic will of the Superior—in order that the will of the Superior may continue to have its "magic power" which must never be questioned. Precisely this is the greatest lie, for the will of the Superior is not supposed to have any power but the power of Christ's humility and of His love.[9]

9. *Turning Towards the World: The Journals of Thomas Merton*, ed. Victor A. Kramer (New York: HarperCollins, 1996) 4:46-47. What Merton learned as a monk nearly always has a relevance for the rest of us because we share the same humanity. Too often the meaning of the will of God has been preached and explained by clergy and vowed religious, whose approach to obedience can tend to be a bit fundamentalist. That is what Merton is reacting to in this 1960 journal entry.

No One Stands in for Jesus

Paul believed that the ground of his own authority as an apostle was nothing less than "Jesus Christ our Lord" (Rom 1:5) or "the will of God" (1 Cor 1:1; 2 Cor 1:1; Eph 1:1). He writes: "Paul an apostle—sent neither by human commission nor from human authorities, but through Jesus Christ and God the Father, who raised him from the dead" (Gal 1:1). The actual religious experience upon which this conviction was based is both intriguing and complex, but in the end Paul's readers would have to trust his experience if they were going to accept his claims.[10] From Paul's side, the truth of his claims had been confirmed by the works of the Spirit that were transforming the communities to which he preached. Paradoxically those claims received further confirmation from the suffering Paul underwent as a consequence of his preaching the gospel and testifying to Jesus as the risen Lord.[11] Suffering for the gospel is a privilege, a mark of divine favor; it indicated that the apostle had been given a share in the cross of Jesus, or to follow an Ignatian image, that the Father had placed him with his Son.[12]

Nevertheless, a naive reading of Paul's statements could lead a person to conclude that one human being can directly represent the voice of God for another. While in no way discounting the multiple ways in which human beings are occasions of grace for each other—for there is a sense in which the mystery of God reaches out from us to others through words, gestures, example, fidelity, and so forth—we need to be cautious not to move from the way we sacramentalize God in countless indirect ways into thinking that we can actually represent God directly for someone else.

Although the Son of Man says in the famous judgment scene "just as you did it to one of the least of these who are members of my family, you did it to me" (Matt 25:40), the evangelist is not suggesting that thirsty, imprisoned, hungry, sick, homeless, or naked messengers of the gospel are

---

10. See John H. Schütz, *Paul and the Anatomy of Apostolic Authority* (Cambridge: Cambridge University Press, 1975).

11. See James D. G. Dunn, *Jesus and the Spirit: A Study of the Religious and Charismatic Experience of Jesus and the First Christians as Reflected in the New Testament* (Philadelphia: The Westminster Press, 1975) 326–38.

12. "One day, a few miles before reaching Rome, he was at prayer in a church and experienced such a change in his soul and saw so clearly that God the Father placed him with Christ his Son that he would not dare doubt it—that God the Father had placed him with his Son." (*The Autobiography*, no. 96.) See *Ignatius of Loyola: Spiritual Exercises and Selected Works*, ed. George E. Ganss (Mahwah, N.J.: Paulist Press, 1991) 109.

actually Jesus in disguise. Similarly, Jesus would say further, "whoever receives one whom I send receives me; and whoever receives me receives
him who sent me" (John 13:20). Nevertheless, he was not claiming that
he actually was the Father. An outright, unqualified identification of Jesus
with the Father simply does not occur in the New Testament.[13]

Divine solidarity with the human condition in its existential poverty
and moral frailty is a key element in our understanding of the incarnation. Solidarity—divine closeness—is what makes the incarnation so spiritually compelling and religiously attractive. Paul could describe Jesus as
the one who, though rich, became poor for our sake.[14] He could write further of the one who did not know sin becoming sin, again for our sake.[15]
Paul was hardly suggesting that Jesus was spiritually impoverished or
morally disabled the way Adam was or that we are. Yet at the same time,
Jesus was one of us and knew the human condition as only people of faith
can. As a result, I would argue that texts which identify Jesus with other
human beings are not "pretend" texts; they are not asking us to make believe that Jesus is the poor person in front of us, or the stranger, or the persecuted one. Instead, they reflect the deep evangelical conviction that God
in Christ has joined the human story and put on the raiment of humanity
at its social and economic worst.

13. Thus the Fourth Gospel announces: "No one has ever seen God. It is God the only Son, who
is close to the Father's heart, who has made him known" (John 1:18). While this differentiation between Jesus and the Father is thematized throughout the entire Gospel, John 14–15 are particularly
illuminating in this regard. Although Jesus says, "Whoever has seen me has seen the Father" (John
14:8), he also states unequivocally, "the Father is greater than I" (14:28). The Jesus of our faith—the
risen Lord—has obviously been portrayed by this evangelist as an icon or sacrament of the Father.
When he claims "The Father and I are one" (10:30), Jesus is speaking of his union with God in the
way that a disciple becomes one with (but not the same person as) Jesus. It is highly unlikely, however, that Jesus portrayed himself this way during his ministry. One way around the christological im-
passe created by the fact that we have these two different portrayals, one that starts with the paschal
mystery and the other that starts with the human, historical Jesus of Nazareth, is to see how the resurrection "completes" the incarnation. According to this view, every theologically adequate christology starts "from above," that is, from a paschal perspective. To separate what Jesus is at the beginning
of the story from what he is at the end would break the logic of faith and ignore Christian religious
experience. This means, therefore, that during his ministry, in the eyes of his contemporaries, Jesus
did not directly represent God for anybody. Similar care must be exercised in interpreting the word
"equal" in John 5:18. An encounter with the risen Lord is at the same time an encounter with God.
The risen Jesus does what God does—he saves and gives life. The equivalence in 5:18 thus appears to
be functional. Likewise, no one can directly represent Jesus. On this point see Edward Kilmartin, *The
Eucharist in the West: History and Theology*, ed. Robert J. Daly (Collegeville, Minn.: The Liturgical
Press, 1998) 348–49, 375–79.
14. 2 Cor 8:9.
15. 2 Cor 5:21.

Jesus is never identified with sinners the way he is identified, say, with those who are prisoners or refugees (although even in the classic case of the judgment scene in Matthew 25 the point seems to be about Jesus' oneness with his messengers and disciples rather than with the poor, the homeless, or the sick as such[16]). We find Jesus consistently in the company of sinners, as in the waters of the Jordan or when he takes meals with them; the Gospels regularly locate him in the company of the sick, the ritually unclean, the demon-possessed, or the chronically hungry. But the evangelists do not equate him with any of these individuals or groups. To make the point clear, Matthew quotes from Second Isaiah:

> That evening they brought to him many who were possessed with demons; and he cast out the spirits with a word, and cured all who were sick. This was to fulfill what had been spoken through the prophet Isaiah, "He took our infirmities and bore our diseases" (Matt 8:16-17).

Picking our way through the thickets of literary forms and convictions of faith in the Bible is not an easy task, primarily because the Bible contains so much narrative, and narrative—stories—combine almost indiscriminately faith, history, imagination, experience, and theology. The four Gospels are complex narratives. While they obviously have to be read devoutly and contemplatively if the voice of the evangelists is to reach us, they must also be read with some comprehension of their literary details. Faith nourishes faith: the reader draws life from the faith of the evangelists. But the pathway to deeper, firmer faith can be blocked if the head is not permitted to join in the search. I do not mean simply that ignorance of history, the Hebrew Bible, and literary forms impedes our comprehension of the gospel texts; that point should be pretty evident. A limited or uninformed understanding of scriptural texts, however, can affect the way we relate to God.

Although the Bible may be the major determinant for how we image and experience God, it is by no means the only influence informing our imagination and shaping our understanding. If we were to confine our understanding of God to what we read in scriptural texts, then our ability

---

16. See Daniel J. Harrington, *The Gospel of Matthew*, Sacra Pagina Series, 1 (Collegeville, Minn.: The Liturgical Press, 1991) 358. Acts 9:4 should probably be approached the same way. The words of the risen Jesus, "Saul, Saul, why do you persecute me?" presuppose Jesus' oneness with his sisters and brothers who constitute the Church. The text is not talking about Jesus' oneness with all victims—that message, I believe, belongs to the mystery of the Cross. Acts 9:4 implies that Jesus' followers bear a marked likeness to Jesus insofar as they are being persecuted for doing what God wants.

to experience God would be narrowed considerably. But the Church never finds God exclusively in its texts and rituals for at least two reasons. First, more often than not life exceeds the language we use to talk about it. This does not result from the insufficiency of human words but from the sheer excess of life over language. And second, in interpreting Scripture we do not simply play one text off against another; the texts, rather, have to play against our experience, and not all our experience is religious. Scripture plays against the world.

Consider, for example, the stories about Moses, the figure whose shadow perhaps more than anyone else's stretches across the Gospels. Moses is presented as the one who spoke directly, regularly, and familiarly with God. Thus whatever Moses relayed to the people was practically by definition the word of God. Now, few of us would subscribe to the belief that God actually dictated his message to Moses from the clouds; we are much more likely to locate the origin of the divine instructions and commands within the human world. Much of what is portrayed as revelation "from above" is essentially a human construction. But the Spirit is an intimate part of the human scene, working through history, culture, everyday events, and above all through the human mind and imagination. The vitality and balance of our interior lives is jeopardized whenever that ordinary working of the Spirit is overlooked and instead we look for solace in fictionalized or supernaturally touched-up accounts of divine action in our world. Popular piety or devotion is one thing; yearning for the spectacular is something else.[17]

Yet the Moses narrative continues to exert a powerful influence, less on our minds than on our imaginations. For the idea that God dealt so directly and immediately with Moses, and subsequently with the prophets, is reassuring in the measure that the rest of us cannot lay claim to similar encounters with God. *Some* individuals, we assure ourselves, were on intensely familiar terms with the divine mystery, even if we are not—at least not to the same degree. One part of us is prepared to concede the interventionist character of revelation suggested by the biblical narratives because the occurrence of miracles stimulates and seems to confirm faith.

17. Readers can reach their own judgment about how and to what extent popular religiosity hinders or promotes an individual's encounter with God. An enlightening and immensely interesting study is Robert A. Orsi, *Thank You, St. Jude: Women's Devotion to the Patron Saint of Hopeless Causes* (New Haven: Yale University Press, 1996). See also Carl Dehne, "Popular Devotions," in *The New Dictionary of Sacramental Worship*, ed. Peter Fink (Collegeville, Minn.: The Liturgical Press, 1990) 331–40.

Moreover, the readiness of many people to accept miraculous interventions of God plays into the willingness of others to position themselves in the role of intermediaries. Another part of us, however, realizes that a faith borrowed from others or induced by wonders rests on an insecure foundation. Believing on the basis of somebody else's word will not sustain us for the long haul, which may explain why the Samaritan villagers declared, "It is no longer because of what you said that we believe, for we have heard for ourselves" (John 4:42). Finally, if the stories about privileged communications from God were to become normative for how divine self-revelation occurs, the vast majority of believers would find themselves relegated to second-class status at best.

The obedience of vowed religious, to return to an earlier point, should never be promoted in a way that would make the word or voice of a superior into a word or voice of God, and the claim ought to be generalized to include all believers. I am not insinuating that people routinely identify what human religious authorities say with the word of God itself; I have no idea to what extent that may be true. Authorities, however, have to be careful not to conflate human tradition with revelation and thereby "make void the word of God" (Matt 15:6). Besides, people are likely to give their assent to a teaching, a directive, an idea in a sermon, or a word of spiritual counsel on the basis of whether or not it conforms to their experience, moves their hearts and imaginations, challenges their thinking, and so on.

Not to Confuse Seeking God with Searching for the Divine Will

Looking for God and looking for the will of God are not the same thing. For many of us, however, the difference is easy to gloss over. We can slide from wanting to grow in our relationship with God into asking God to clarify what precisely we are expected to do or how we are supposed to live. A not uncommon dissatisfaction with simply being or living in God's presence springs perhaps from a culturally ingrained conviction that to be worthwhile we always have to be accomplishing something; or from a religiously ingrained conviction that salvation requires both faith and works; or from a biblically supported conviction that the God revealed in the history of Israel and the life of Jesus is a God who acts and not just silently meditates or passively observes. The practice of faith unfolds over a continuum that stretches from pure or total contemplation to total action. The rarefied poles of the continuum are pure abstractions, of course, in whose atmosphere no mature Christian will long survive. But the contemplative/active distinction does point to one of the complexities within Christian religious experience. Love of God and love or service of our neighbor belong together not only because love expresses itself in deeds but also because God is experienced in acts of love and encountered in the peoples of the world.

In a most general way, of course, we already know how God wants us to conduct ourselves; the ethical aspect of the will of God is clear. We have the moral teaching of the Bible, the evangelical ideal Jesus set forth in the Sermon on the Mount and elsewhere in the Gospels, and the teaching of the Church. And to assure us that we shall have the ability to transpose Jesus' teaching into a contemporary key, the Fourth Gospel underscores the fact that Jesus' followers have been granted the gift of the Spirit who will teach them all things (John 15:26; 16:7, 13). Beyond these articulations of the divine will in our regard, however, many writers draw attention to the wholesome desires planted in the human heart, presumably by the Spirit.[18] Identifying and understanding these desires, prioritizing them when necessary, and allowing them to shape one's future—that is the business normally associated with spiritual direction. Learning how to differentiate between healthy and unhealthy desires and inclinations is an important but rudimentary lesson for those who are trying to understand and deepen their relationship with God. Learning how to differentiate what is good from what is better presupposes a sharper sensitivity to the action of the Spirit and a fairly sophisticated (although not necessarily articulated) grasp of how one's life fits into the grand scheme of God's creative designs for the world. In other words, sensitivity to the Spirit presumes that a person has grown theologically—not in an academic or curricular sense, yet in a sense that definitely involves reason, intelligence, and judgment.

That God is at work in human history and within individual lives is a central claim of Christian faith, but exactly *how* God is involved is far less clear. The New Testament speaks comfortably and with great frequency of an ongoing interaction between heaven and earth, between God and

---

18. See, for instance, Denis Donoghue, "God's Will: Where Desires Commingle," *Review for Religious* 60:6 (2001) 647–54. Also, Janet K. Ruffing, *Spiritual Direction: Beyond the Beginnings* (Mahwah, N.J.: Paulist Press, 2000) 9–31.

human beings, between the Spirit and the Church, and so on. I often wonder about how much human religious energy would be conserved if only God were to act directly and unmistakably in our lives and world, in much the same way that divine initiative is portrayed in a wide variety of biblical passages. Experience and common sense have taught us, however, not to read those texts too literally, since taking them literally creates unrealistic expectations of how God should act in our own life and times. For believers, on the one hand divine engagement with human lives cannot be perceived without faith: faith enables us to see the finger of God at work in the world. Yet on the other hand it is faith that makes divine action possible. Thus Jesus would say, "Daughter, your faith has made you well" (Mark 5:34), or "All things can be done for the one who believes" (Mark 9:23).

Once we lay aside any craving for wondrous encounters, the next best thing might be to be on the lookout for heavenly signs. Lacking the directness and immediacy of an encounter with Jesus like the one Paul was granted on the road to Damascus,[19] we would gladly welcome divine action working indirectly, provided, of course, that we have first been able to discern the hand of God moving, shaping, and directing our lives and our history. People are likely to approach a spiritual director for assistance in discerning the motion of God's hand for the simple reason that divine action is normally not all that evident or self-explanatory. Thus Paul advises the Thessalonians to "test everything" (1 Thess 5:21) and John urges his community to "test the spirits to see whether they are from God" (1 John 4:1).

That historical events and divine intention cannot be separated is a feature of biblical faith—I am thinking, for example, of the book of Wisdom—but divine purpose is never immediately obvious to the untrained eye. In a way reminiscent of the patriarch who proved so adept at interpreting dreams,[20] Joseph—Mary's husband—was visited by an angelic interpreter while he slept.[21] And the heavenly messenger who opened Daniel's eyes to the political fortunes of an empire that was persecuting the people of God provided a prophetic template for the author of Revelation as he contemplated the arrogance and pagan decadence of imperial Rome. We are, of course, religiously smart enough to realize that decisions

---

19. Acts 9:1ff.
20. See Gen 39–41.
21. Matt 1:20, 2:13, 2:19, 2:22.

ought not to be made by consulting the Urim and Thummim,[22] by casting lots,[23] by reading too much into coincidences, or even by letting a finger fall randomly on some passage of Scripture. And we are equally familiar enough with the ways of God not to waste time begging for an angelic visitor or recalling dreams as if they were divine oracles.

Even though we speak rather loosely about accepting whatever God wills, our references to the will of God ought to be circumspect. To start with, we have a comprehensive view of life, believing that God has called us into existence and that God daily creates us—or redeems us or makes us holy—insofar as we respond to the overtures of divine grace. Thus whenever we pray "Your will be done," we are both confessing this most fundamental of religious beliefs and asking God to help us respond ever more generously and fearlessly to God's creative, redeeming, transforming action in our personal lives as well as in the world. "Your will be done" is a prayer that acknowledges divine sovereignty and yearns for deeper intimacy with the One who is the source of all love and holiness. This prayer takes on the note of surrender when we find ourselves in circumstances totally beyond our control, like the prophetic Jesus nailed to the cross and unable to accomplish anything further by way of preaching or healing. "We must work the works of him who sent me while it is day," the evangelist recalls Jesus saying; "night is coming when no one can work" (John 9:4). But "Your will be done" should also be heard as a declaration of prophetic commitment: we earnestly want God's will to unfold on earth and we are prepared to do all that is in our power to establish justice, faith, and peace in this world. "Your will be done" becomes the words of a Christian activist, an energetic disciple, an evangelist of a community conscious of its mission.

In brief, then, God "wills" the redemption of the human race. Consequently, the responsibility of women and men to listen to God's word and put it into practice translates into their embracing a lifelong process of conversion and growth. In that process they open themselves—or rather they allow the Spirit to open them—to the transformative power of divine love. Our tradition attests over and over again that this process will entail asceticism and suffering, for these realities play an integral role in our coming to know and embrace the mystery of God. In the memorable words of the let-

22. Exod 28:30; Lev 8:8; Deut 33:8; Ezra 2:63.
23. Acts 1:26.

ter to the Hebrews, "Although he was a Son, he learned obedience through what he suffered; and having been made perfect, he became the source of eternal salvation for all who obey him" (Heb 5:8-9). Obedience in this context ought not to be read as a humble surrender to painful events which God had ordained. I think the text makes a stronger impact when obedience is understood as Jesus' readiness to feel the intensity of divine love for the world—a love that seeks only to rescue and save, to heal and restore, to set free and to caress. Jesus—"the reflection of God's glory and the exact imprint of God's very being" (Heb 1:3)—had first to experience divine salvation, the transforming force of God's love for the world, before he could become a pattern of life or source of salvation for others. Consequently, the idea of obeying Jesus in Hebrews 5:9 amounts to opening oneself to the onrush of divine affection which comes from living in, with, and from his Spirit.

To repeat, we need to be wary of any suggestion that God's will consists of a calling or plan that we are meant to uncover. For when looked at this way human beings are bound to be frustrated, since we shall never know for certain whether we have really figured out what God wants of us. Indeed, in matters pertaining to God, all "knowing" is the knowing of faith, the knowing that is interwoven with trust and belief. In other words, whatever we think God has planned for us could not be known with greater certainty than whatever knowledge of God we have in the first place. Believers hardly have more grounds for being sure of the state of life to which they feel called, for example, than they have for being sure about the mystery of God itself. Sometimes people sound more confident that they are doing what God wants than they are of the existence of God.

I realize that the sense of being called often confirms a person's experience of God, since God both "is" and "acts": knowing God and experiencing oneself as "called" by God may be viewed as two sides of a single spiritual coin. In the process of reflection knowing God and being called by God might appear to be distinct moments, but I would urge that they are really part of a single experience. In fact, there are probably a number of other aspects as well. Being called and experiencing oneself as sent would be another part. For the sense of being called implies a fundamental mission in life that gets spelled out in terms of being called to "praise, reverence, and serve God our Lord"[24] in large measure by working, praying, and living for others.

---

24. See No. 23 in the Spiritual Exercises, the Principle and Foundation.

Knowing God means knowing God as the Lord and giver of life; it means experiencing oneself as "called" into existence and, therefore, as loved. And so on. Yet the point remains: we are not going to be more certain of the *basic* calling of our lives (which we become sensitive to the more we reflect on the fact that we exist at all) than we are of God's real presence in our lives and world. And we certainly should be concerned whenever vocational choices—particular responses to divine action in one's life—with their reassuring routine and predictability start to feel more secure or certain than our awareness of the divine mystery itself. If a person's relatedness to God becomes static, there may be a temptation to take refuge in one's "vocation," one's work. But where our relatedness to God is dynamic and alive, then the concrete form of our vocational choices remains supple, even open to the possibility of being re-formed. I take this to be the insight behind Jesus' words about new wine necessitating new wineskins.[25] Or his words to Nicodemus about being born—and I would insert "continually"—from above.[26]

New Testament Imaging of the Action of God

Of all the religious influences that shape the way we think about God, God's way of relating to us, and how God moves in our lives, the New Testament writings are in all likelihood the most formative. For their theology of God, needless to say, the New Testament writers in general assumed for their point of departure the Hebrew Scriptures, which affirm that

> God's work and God's word are expressions of God's will, and all God's creatures experience the effects of this divine will. God wills to be involved in all the world in creation and redemption. . . .
>
> All creation and its life is continually grounded in and permeated by the providential will of God; it remains within the scope of the ongoing divine will of blessing for the world. As such, the creative order witnesses to God's will for the world; it is a source of Israel's knowledge of that will. Moreover, because God does not confine God's willing activity to the people of Israel, God's will is experienced and known, at least in part, in places where God's name is not explicitly confessed.[27]

25. Mark 2:22.
26. John 3:3.
27. Terrence E. Fretheim, "Will of God in the OT," in *The Anchor Bible Dictionary*, ed. David Noel Freedman (New York: Doubleday, 1992) 6:918. Fretheim includes "promise" and "salvation" in the same section of his entry ("Experiencing the Will of God"). In other words, Israel *experienced* God as promise and fidelity, and as salvation; these notions are basic aspects of Israel's creation theology.

The biblical God creates, sees, hears, touches, calls, gives birth, promises, speaks, legislates, threatens, punishes, rescues, heals, forgives, teaches, guides, restores, judges, rewards, makes holy, raises the dead—and reigns. The presence of so many verbs reminds us of what may be the overarching divine "predicate"—the biblical God is imaged as forever acting. As Origen noted in the third century, the biblical God never ceases to be the Creator or Maker, the Parent of the universe.[28] In addition to the verbs we have a variety of metaphors. Like the verbs, the metaphors reveal aspects of the way that the people of Israel had experienced God: "Metaphors are used to unite the conceptual and the experiential in the knowledge of the faithful God. The Lord is rock, refuge, fortress, strength and shield, shepherd, light, guide to right paths—all images that invite trust."[29]

Given the persistence of the scriptural idea that God is by nature (at least from our perspective) active and given how the human response to God's word so frequently follows a prophetic pattern, it is somewhat remarkable that Christian spirituality developed such a strong contemplative tradition. The religious and cultural forces that conspired to evoke a more contemplative, even solitary way of life among some Christians do not appear to have been modeled on anything we regularly come across in the Bible. This is not to say that biblical figures did not meditate, ponder, or occasionally seclude themselves, as when Elijah retreated to Mount Horeb or Jesus to the wilderness. But as increasing attention was paid to the prayerful pursuit of God in, for example, the ancient monastic communities that sprang up in the desert or in the "negative theology" of writers like Gregory of Nyssa, the biblical image of God would be modified on the basis of a particular type of religious experience. The Bible never functioned in the everyday life of the Church independently of the social and cultural conditions in which Christian communities found themselves, but sometimes those conditions may have filtered out important scriptural perspectives on the God of life.

More to the point, however, they shed light on the religious experience of a people. God is not simply one who makes a promise; God is faithfulness and faithfulness in one's individual history as well as in the history of the people is what was experienced. God is not simply the one who saves; God is salvation—and wholeness, restoration, defeat of enemies, redress of wrongs, mercy, and inner consolation are what was experienced.

28. See Origen, *On First Principles*, bk. 1, ch. 4, trans. G. W. Butterworth (Gloucester, Mass.: Peter Smith, 1973) 41–43.

29. See James Luther Mays, "The God Who Reigns," in A. Andrew Das and Frank J. Matera, eds., *The Forgotten God: Perspectives in Biblical Theology* (Louisville, Ky.: Westminster John Knox Press, 2002) 34.

When human beings want to speak about God they necessarily have recourse to a distinctive language of symbol and metaphor. Although each of us believes that God is really at work in human lives and that God becomes present to people in a wide variety of ways, in general we would not maintain that the language describing the divine presence and action ought to be interpreted literally. Bearing this in mind, it would be good for us to review some of the ways in which the New Testament images the action of God both in our world and in human lives.

1. First and foremost, God is the one who raises the dead and the premier illustration of this divine action is the raising of Jesus. What "raising the dead" means, however, is by no means immediately clear. The great prophetic text of Ezekiel 37 presents a scene in which bones reassemble, gather flesh and sinew, and receive anew God's lifegiving spirit. But the scene is evidently a metaphor for the restoration of Israel, not an announcement to be taken literally. When the Sadduccees quarreled with Jesus over the resurrection of the dead, he responded that they knew neither Scripture nor the power of God.[30] Jesus believed that at the right time God could and would "raise the dead," though the Gospel leaves unexplained what exactly this raising of the dead will look like. For that speculation one would have to turn to 1 Thessalonians 4:13-18.

We are hardly in a position to question Jesus whether his belief in the raising of the dead concerned the immortality of the individual or the ultimate victory of God's justice over all the forces of violence and greed. It can be argued, however, that to confess that at the end of the age the dead will be raised is basically an expression of life-determining hope and trust in God couched in apocalyptic terms. In other words, to believe in the raising of the dead was a way of insisting that human history ultimately answers to God—the God of life, since God is not God for the dead but for the living. The point is not simply that God makes everlasting life possible but that divine power can and will checkmate and defeat the destructive forces that throughout history have assaulted human beings and their communities, their civilizations and their boldest aspirations. In short, the prospect that the dead will be raised adds very little to our believing in God in the first place. God is by definition, we might say, the one who raises the dead since the God of the New Testament is preeminently the God of life.

30. Mark 12:24-27; Matt 22:29-32.

2. Sometimes divine action in human life is narrated in dramatic terms, as in the story of Paul's encounter with the risen Jesus. Divine action can also be mythologized, as in apocalyptic texts where the basic point is about divine judgment.[31] The providential arrangement of human affairs is certainly hinted at with the two accounts of Jesus' genealogy,[32] in the sense that, for those who love God, all things work out for good.[33] The angels who speak to Mary,[34] to Joseph in his dreams,[35] to the women at the empty tomb,[36] or to the centurion Cornelius;[37] the voice that speaks to Peter when the blanket descended from the heavens with all sorts of foods;[38] the voice of the Lord that assures Paul of the sufficiency of grace in the face of human weakness;[39] and even the heavenly voice we are permitted to hear at the baptism and transfiguration scenes in the life of Jesus[40]—each of these instances indicates the readiness of the New Testament to depict divine engagement with human beings as direct and immediate.

3. In talking about God, Jesus remarks that God sees what is unseen and "feeds" the birds and "clothes" the grass[41]—statements that flow from his own faith in the providential ordering of the world. Indeed, God knows the most minute details about us: "And even the hairs of your head are all counted" (Matt 10:30). The same perspective can be found, of course, in prayers such as Psalm 104 with its celebration of the order and awe-inspiring design which would appear strikingly evident to a person raised in the countryside and close to the natural world.

But providential care can also be seen in the overall sweep of history: "Long ago God spoke to our ancestors in many and various ways by the prophets, but in these last days he has spoken to us by a Son" (Heb 1:1-2). The physical or historical details of that involvement can be discerned in the genealogy of Jesus, for after recounting the generations that led up to

---

31. Mark 13:24-27.
32. Matt 1:1-17; Luke 3:23-38.
33. Rom 8:28.
34. Luke 1:26ff.
35. Matt 1:20-21; 2:13, 19-20.
36. Matt 28:5-7; Luke 24:22-23; John 20:11-13.
37. Acts 10:3ff.
38. Acts 10:13ff.
39. 2 Cor 12:8-9.
40. E.g., Mark 1:11 and 9:7.
41. Matt 6:18; 6:26, 30.

Jesus and the particulars surrounding his birth, the evangelist concluded: "All this took place to fulfill what had been spoken by the Lord" (Matt 1:22). *All this:* starting with Abraham and following the bloodline to Joseph, the gospel text draws our imagination through the multiplicity of events, circumstances, sins, humiliations, adventures, defeats and triumphs that constituted Israel's past and led up to Jesus' birth. Later in the story, when Jesus was coming up from the waters of the Jordan, the divine voice would reconfirm the providential arrangement signified in the genealogy: "This is my Son, the Beloved, with whom I am well pleased" (Matt 3:17).

4. This sense of divine ordering governs the way Luke recounts the story of the early Church. The geographical and temporal range of the narrative stretches from Jerusalem to Rome, but Luke hardly disguises his conviction that the spreading of the gospel involved a lot more than the unfolding of social and cultural forces. After all, there were in antiquity numerous religious movements and spiritual novelties which were carried easily on the winds of commerce and along imperial highways. For the story of Acts is punctuated with over fifty mentions of the Spirit, and it was the presence of the Spirit that differentiated the Way[42] from the cults and philosophies which like weeds had seeded themselves across the empire.

God works surely even if imperceptibly within the actions, fortuitous events, and everyday circumstances that shape our lives, although the presence of God is more immediately discernible in the charismatic bursts of healing, inspired utterance, enthusiasm, heroic generosity, tongues, and prayerfulness that characterized many of the earliest communities. Rather than halting or even destroying the early Christian movement, rejection and persecution served only to make it more vibrant. The early Church had grasped the paschal connection between divine power and human weakness, and it had also discovered that when human hearts are centered on God nothing on earth could prevent their good works from bearing fruit.

5. The verbs listed above that describe divine action in the Hebrew Scriptures are not foreign to the New Testament, but their subject might be the Father, Jesus, the Spirit—or simply God. While there is virtually no divine attribute in the Christian Scriptures that cannot be located in some text of the Hebrew Bible, Paul's claim that faith makes human beings righteous before God is potentially the most challenging, at least

42. See Acts 9:2; 18:25-26; 19:9, 23; 22:4; 24:14, 22.

from the standpoint of spiritual direction. We shall be looking at the distinctiveness of Christian religious experience and the bearing this distinctiveness has upon the ministry of direction in chapters four and five. If we presume that ultimately our destiny consists of a communion with one another in the inexhaustible consolation of union with God—in other words, the mystery of unending love—then whatever brings us closer to that destiny, prepares us for it, or schools us in it belongs to the process of our ongoing creation. Whether we call that process redemption, salvation, reconciliation, justification, sanctification, divinization, and so forth, we are talking essentially about the same thing.

Now if one holds that every righteous person will wind up in the state of blessedness, the various religious "means" by which we get there are going to seem pretty relative. Paul, however, did not draw this conclusion, perhaps because his theology was so Christ-centered. For Paul, Christ is the offspring of Abraham and the ultimate recipient of the divine promise; a person has access to Christ not by virtue of ethnicity but by virtue of faith. Justification, therefore, meant entering into a personal, lifelong relationship of trust and love with the risen Jesus.

But let us suppose for a moment that Jesus had not come or that the gospel had not been preached. In that case justification would default to a personal, lifelong relationship of love and trust with the mystery of God. Men and women who had been schooled in the Psalms and imbued with their spirit could not be considered less justified than those who would have been baptized in Christ Jesus, unless God decided to change the terms of the covenant. And here is our dilemma. Either God introduces something new into the righteousness equation or Jesus is made relative—one of several possible means to the blessedness that awaits the righteous. Neither of these alternatives is intellectually satisfying and, I would suggest, neither does full justice to Christian religious experience. Spiritual directors cannot afford to leave these concerns off the table because at stake is their ministry's fidelity to the paschal experience of the Church.

Chapter 3

Where Do Holy Desires Come From?

That human hearts and minds are oriented toward God and that the chief manifestation of this orientation is desire, yearning, or even passion is generally taken to be an axiom of the interior life. Whether this desiring is construed as the intellect's movement toward truth, the imagination's longing for beauty, the heart's wanting to embrace and to be embraced, *noūs* (Greek: mind) as "the place of God within us,"[1] or Julian of Norwich's "wound of sincere longing,"[2] by centering on desire we describe the human person as someone who seeks fulfillment through a process of self-transcending that unfolds over a lifetime. Desire is the mainspring of human nature. The ultimate object of this process—the end toward which we are constantly striving and steadily moving (provided we are sincerely seeking what is good and wholesome)—is the infinite truth, life, goodness, beauty, and love that we call God.

For most of my adult life I have accepted as self-evident the proposition that desire is the key indicator of what is generally signified by the human "spirit." If you help someone get in touch with this core desire— the native restlessness of the human heart—then you have helped that person on her or his way to God. The desire, once discovered, and the process, once it has been set in motion, will guide or draw a person toward the mystery of God, as if in obedience to a natural instinct. Those women and men who have failed to discover the presence of God in their lives may have resisted the dynamic of the heart's desiring through ignorance or sinfulness, or they may never have had the opportunity to be

---

1. André Louf, *Grace Can Do More* (Kalamazoo, Mich.: Cistercian Publications, 2002) 164.

2. Julian of Norwich, *Revelations of Divine Love*, trans. Clifton Wolters (New York: Penguin Books, 1966) 64.

awakened to the possibility of cultivating an interior life—a possibility or capacity which derives from the fact that we have been made for God, though perhaps not for God "alone." I presumed that our spirituality saw an analogy with our physical or biological constitution: just as our bodies are programmed to reach for whatever promotes physical wellbeing, so mind and heart have been fashioned to search for what will sustain the human spirit. In what pertains to the spirit, however, things behave differently. Whoever makes physical and social wellbeing the primary object of the heart's desire will wind up losing everything.[3] The law governing the growth and development of the human spirit is "counter-intuitive": we are saved by letting go.

Reading the candid narratives in Studs Terkel's *Will the Circle Be Broken?*, however, awakened in me a persistent though normally dormant suspicion about the adequacy of our usual way of thinking about how we are put together.[4] A number of those whom Terkel interviewed confided that while they may have engaged in religious practice when they were younger, they had long since put aside matters of belief and worship. Others disclosed that religion had never been a part of their lives, not even in childhood, and thus they had to deal with mortality, sickness, and physical diminishment with whatever resources life had equipped them. The description of the human person in which I have been steeped intellectually and which I habitually bring to my reading and evaluation of religious writing has not always felt up to the task of making sense of *every* human life. Some human lives seem simply to have fallen out of bounds, as it were. While in the case of some people the sense of God appears to have died, for others it seems never to have been born.

Not all lives wind up in God, at least not in an express or conscious relationship with the divine mystery which, theoretically, should have been accompanying them over the years. The suggestion that the holy mystery of God has been part of those lives in an anonymous or nameless fashion, provided that they have been following their conscience, has not been intellectually satisfying. I do not doubt the mercy or closeness of God, but comforting my mind with the assurance that God is in the picture even for those who pay scant attention to where they came from and where

3. Mark 8:35.
4. Studs Terkel, *Will the Circle Be Broken?: Reflections on Death, Rebirth, and Hunger for a Faith* (New York: New Press, 2001).

they are heading flies in the face of experience. The moral and spiritual stakes are simply too high, as I hope to explain. I readily and gladly concede that the mystery of God far exceeds our humble efforts to think theologically. Furthermore, I know that if God is love then those who have truly loved others during the course of their lives have somehow known God. Nevertheless, my mind rests uncomfortably with the prospect that whether one knows God explicitly or one knows God implicitly ultimately makes little difference. The psalmist wrote many centuries ago:

> The LORD looks down from heaven;
> he sees all humankind.
> From where he sits enthroned he watches
> all the inhabitants of the earth—
> he who fashions the hearts of them all,
> and observes all their deeds. (Ps 33:13-15)

These verses articulate one of my most solid convictions—particularly the words "he who fashions the hearts of them all." Nevertheless, the psalmist can do no more than voice his personal belief; he can speak only from within his experience of what God is like. Not even an inspired writer can make God present to people, even though God fashioned their hearts.

Like all of us the psalmist would have been instructed about God as he learned the prayers of his people and stepped into the images and metaphors of Israel's sacred narratives. Yet Psalm 33 presents not just a way of *conceiving* God; it also invites readers to pay close attention to how the divine mystery has shown itself in their own lives. Or to put the matter differently, atheists do not pray, at least not according to any conventional understanding of prayer. God may have fashioned their hearts and might be observing all their deeds, but what difference does that make to the individual whose heart seems to say that there is no God? Are such people "fools"?[5] Are there people who simply never pine or thirst for God?[6] Is the desire for God like a seed that needs to germinate? On one hand so many believers have testified to the awakening of that desire within them that I hesitate to suggest that perhaps there are people in whom the potential— the seed—is totally absent. Yet on the other hand most of us know at least

5. Pss 14:1; 53:1.
6. Ps 42:1-2.

a few men and women who would never characterize themselves as having a deficient interior life because they do not pray to or even believe in God.

Another way to consider this question might be to ask whether the desire for God belongs to the way we have been hardwired or whether it is one of several software programs loaded into us, depending upon when and where we were born and raised. Although I like the neatness and simplicity of the first—the desire for God built into the mainframe of our thinking, choosing and loving—the second explanation may be truer to experience. It would also make preaching and witness absolutely essential to the awareness of God both with respect to the individual and to society at large. Recall what Paul wrote:

> But how are they to call on one in whom they have not believed? And how are they to believe in one of whom they have never heard? And how are they to hear without someone to proclaim him? . . . So faith comes from what is heard, and what is heard comes through the word of Christ (Rom 10:14, 17).

Now Paul had also stated that in the case of the Gentiles "what the law requires is written on their hearts, to which their own conscience also bears witness" (Rom 2:15). In a more fundamental way, Paul believed that the divine nature and power were reflected in the very creation of the world (Rom 1:20)—what can be known about God is plain to those who "by their wickedness suppress the truth" (1:19). He is claiming that the moral law is not extrinsic to human nature and the basis of his claim was the experience of conscience: we feel the tension, the pull, the drive toward self-consistency associated with the difference between good an evil. Paul is claiming further that the universe around us is constantly emitting signals about the existence of God and the kind of God who must be responsible for what we observe around us. Yet these claims are not about faith. Rather, Paul is giving us a sort of phenomenological sketch of human nature.

The reason for exploring Paul's conclusion that "faith comes from what is heard" is that we are forced to think about the absolute necessity of a climate or culture of faith if there is to be any hearing. The desire for God, it seems to me, is not so much awakened as implanted. Faith is our response to the word preached to us, but the preaching is layered with witness—the conviction and insight of the one preaching, the integrity of the preacher's manner of living, the depth of his or her insertion into the life of a Christian community, prayerfulness, joy, and liberty of heart, compassion, an unfailing love for one's sisters and brothers. Whether through direct contact with men and women who are genuinely people of faith or through indirect contact with them through their writing or through accounts of their lives, our searching for God simply has to unfold within a climate of belief. In my experience, people do not just stumble onto God, more or less the way Moses did when he encountered the burning bush. The atmosphere of faith may at times be quite thin, but without some exposure to belief it is difficult to see how the word "God" would acquire any practical significance. Preaching, then, is not so much what awakens a latent orientation toward the divine as it is a way of seeding the human world with "words of God." Through preaching—complemented obviously by the vibrant witness of Christian communities—a new social reality is made possible: the faith-world, where men and women discover a way of being human together that is both appealing and distinctive.

I have stressed the idea that the desire for God is implanted rather than awakened, that it comes from exposure to a culture of faith rather than from the mind's own hardware, because spiritual direction cannot produce rabbits from hats. No one can generate a religious experience for somebody else, as if to say, "You see? God has been in there all the time!" There is a tendency to look inwards when we ought to be looking out, to self-examine and self-analyze when we should be paying more attention to faith as a dimension of social reality. Karl Rahner's analysis of the human being starts with a description of the transcendence to be found within human nature. After all, human beings would not be able to encounter and receive the mystery of God into their lives (and God by definition is transcendence itself) unless by their very constitution they were receptors of the divine. The word "God" itself points to the correlation that exists between human capacity and divine gift, between human receptivity and divine word, or between human longing and divine object of the heart's desiring.[7]

As impressive as this description of the human being sounds, however, I do not find it a persuasive basis on which to erect a theology of spiritual direction. Consider, for instance, our experience of apologetics, that is, of attempting to demonstrate to others the reasonableness and truth of Christian faith. While the instruction of 1 Peter 3:15 is as relevant today as it was in the first century—"Always be ready to make your defense to

---

7. See, for example, Karl Rahner, *The Content of Faith: The Best of Karl Rahner's Theological Writings* (New York: The Crossroad Publishing Co., 1992) 205–26.

anyone who demands from you an accounting for the hope that is in you"—human hearts do not surrender in faith to God on the basis of reasonableness and logic alone. That insufficiency helps to account for why attempts to "prove" the existence of God turn out to be pastorally and spiritually frustrating. However compelling arguments for God's existence may appear, based as they are on our necessarily limited perception of order, design, and beauty in the universe, the fact is that such demonstrations of themselves do not lead non-believers, skeptics, and agnostics to kneel and adore. Hence the often repeated observation that for those without faith no amount of argument will be sufficient while for those with faith no argument is necessary. Rahner's description of the human being is attractive from the perspective of an intellectual or philosophical aesthetics. But as the categories used to think about God become more philosophical, they also become less interesting from the perspective of ordinary experience. I am also left with the uneasy feeling that Rahner's individualistic philosophical starting point paves the way for God to be viewed as a projection of human transcendence.

The church is not a collectivity of individual God-seekers who need temporary support as they walk their private routes toward eternity. Although the church like any institution certainly has its own particular structure and while many people have had issues with the church precisely because of the way its structure sometimes behaves, its institutional aspect is but one element of a larger and richer reality. What first comes to mind when I think of the church is family life, since home was where my faith was taught, modeled, nurtured and confirmed. Who would eat without saying Grace or go to bed without night prayers? What home would not have a crucifix, a picture or statue of Mary, a nativity arrangement, a bottle of holy water, or a blessed candle? We learned about virtue by watching it in the adult Christians around us.

I next think of the Liturgy, with its calendar and reassuring cycle of saints and feasts, and the church's rich devotional life. I think of prayer and the lifelong cultivation of a habit of mindfulness of God's presence. I think of clergy and religious, of outdoor shrines and church buildings. I think of great missionary enterprises, countless works of mercy and of love, schools, hospitals, orphanages, soup kitchens, radio stations, cooperatives, printing presses. I think of martyrs, mystics, and prophets, but also of scholars, scientists, philosophers, artists, musicians, and inventors.

Finally, I think of preaching and in that preaching what remains most impressive had little to do with promoting morality and much to do with retelling the story of Jesus. In the end, the birth and development of faith is a product of imagination, where imagination means putting on the Christian story—living inside the gospel and understanding the mystery of God through the life and death of Jesus. Church is the atmosphere in which we feel, think, judge, and act; we breathe it. Where such an atmosphere is lacking, the search for God is going to resemble a philosopher's search for truth and enlightenment—Magi without a star.

The desire for God, then, is a particular configuration of human longing that springs from within the human world. We do not depreciate this desire by drawing attention to its cultural, social, and communal determinants. It does not appear that we are born with an innate desire for God, but this is not to say that there is nothing spiritual about us, either. Intellect and will, imagination, heart, and memory are the obvious elements one thinks of in the effort to explain what makes us "spiritual." And the spiritual side of us both needs cultivation and craves expression. But to repeat, I do not believe that a study of the history of religion warrants the conclusion that the idea of God is a priori to the human heart and mind. That religion was a major feature of life in the ancient world, that it manifested nearly endless variety, and that it remains vitally important to many people today is demonstrably true. That human beings cannot survive without religion in their lives or that the absence of religion inevitably leads to gross immorality or social chaos is demonstrably false. Besides, religion itself has hardly been immune to the effects of original sin.

Once it leaves the primeval garden, biblical theology resolves somewhat the matter about where the idea of God comes from by having the divine mystery reveal itself to Abraham, then in a privileged way to Moses, and finally in various ways to the prophets. Since there is no God except the LORD—Israel's God—then the gods of the nations are of absolutely no account; in the end they do not exist—or, as James Kugel put it, they had been fired for incompetence.[8] Clearly, for biblical writers the notion of "god" is an empty notion, so that the only way for us to know

8. Kugel writes: "what Psalm 82 is saying is that, some long time ago, God (here meaning the God of Israel) stood up in the *'adat 'el*, the council of the gods, and fired everyone. . . . Because the gods had failed to administer justice properly . . . they were no longer fit to be gods." See *The God of Old: Inside the Lord World of the Bible* (New York: The Free Press, 2003) 123.

the LORD is for the LORD to "come down to deliver" (Exod 3:8). In salvation history the desire for God is more accurately a desire for the LORD, but there is no way of learning about the LORD that bypasses Israel as the chosen people. The nations must come to Israel. What leads them to come, in Isaiah's vision, is not an abstract philosophical or theological quest, but the wisdom and holiness surrounding a particular community of faith.[9]

In short, I do not think the desire for God can be separated from a desire to be with God's people. The desire for God is a way of naming an intense longing on the part of some men and women to share in the life of the one human family that God created. This is not by any means to deify humanity; it is simply to notice that the life of God and the life of God's people have always run together. The phrase "desire for God"—part longing, part hope—is a way of envisioning a particular sort of person, a distinctive way of being in the world. And we learn what "God" means, in much the same way we learn about everything else, from a community that has a story to tell. Whatever good and holy desires we have, like every other blessing in life, come from God. But the language of holy desire and blessing supposes a framework of faith. Those living outside of that framework may view themselves as fortunate, perhaps as recipients of civic blessing; but they obviously are not going to be praising God for the goodness they enjoy. The desire for God, I would conclude, is essentially an ecclesial desire—a desire rendered possible by the existence of a community of faith. We may not have been born *with* this desire, but if those around us are believers we are certainly born *into* it. As soon as someone sits down with a spiritual director, she or he has stepped into a faith-world, however slender or tenuous the threads that are drawing that world close.

No Finding without Seeking

Do people find God? The answer, of course, is yes, although it may not always be immediately clear what they mean when they say they have found God.[10] In a moving testament for Jesuits today in which he had as-

9. E.g., Isa 42:1-9; 56:3-8; 60:1-22. The same conviction runs through the psalms that celebrate God's gift of the law. For example, see Ps 19:7-10.

10. See James Martin, ed., *How Can I Find God?: The Famous and Not-So-Famous Consider the Quintessential Question* (Ligouri, Mo.: Triumph Books, 1997). The book is immensely interesting,

sumed the voice of Ignatius addressing the Society four centuries after his death, Karl Rahner wrote:

> When I claim to have known God first hand, I do not intend here to add to my assertion a theological treatise on the nature of such a direct experience of God, nor a catalogue of all the accompanying phenomena of such an experience, which naturally have their own characteristics both personal and historical. . . All I say is I knew God, nameless and unfathomable, silent and yet near, bestowing himself upon me in his Trinity, I knew God beyond all concrete imaginings. I knew Him clearly in such nearness and grace as is impossible to confound or mistake. . . .
>
> I truly encountered God, the living and true God, who merits this name which supersedes all other names. Whether such an experience is mystical or not is irrelevant here; how it is at all possible to make such an experience comprehensible using human concepts is for your theologians to speculate. . . . I encountered God, I knew him. . . .
>
> God himself: I knew God himself, not simply human words describing him. I knew God and the freedom which is an integral part of him and which can only be known through him and not as the sum total of finite realities and calculations about them.[11]

Rahner's claim could not be clearer; knowing God is categorically different from knowing any*thing* or any*one* else. But the sentiment sounds more like Rahner than Ignatius; behind it lies a lifetime of intellectually exploring the ground of faith. More familiar to most of us might be the opening paragraphs of *The Confessions* where Augustine reflects on the dynamics of seeking and finding:

> 'Grant me Lord to know and understand' which comes first—to call upon you or to praise you, and whether knowing you precedes calling upon you. But who calls upon you when he does not know you? For an ignorant person might call upon someone else instead of the right one. But surely you may be called upon in prayer that you may be known. Yet 'how shall they call upon him in whom they have not believed? and how shall they believe without a preacher?' 'They will praise the Lord who seek for him'.
>
> In seeking him they find him, and in finding him they will praise him. Lord, I would seek you, calling upon you—and calling upon you is an act

---

but one wonders what exactly led some of the contributors to associate God with the experiences or situations they related.

11. Karl Rahner and Paul Imhof, *Ignatius of Loyola* (London: Collins, 1979) 11, 12.

of believing in you. You have been preached to us. My faith, Lord, calls upon you. It is your gift to me. You breathed it into me by the humanity of your Son, by the ministry of your preacher.[12]

In general it can be said that the experience of finding God is very much connected to what we are first looking for. The one who discovered a treasure buried in a field appears to have come upon it accidentally, but the merchant who found the pearl of great value had been on the lookout for some time. Still, a case could be made that no one "goes and sells all that he has and buys that field" (Matt 13:44) whose heart had not been longing for such extraordinary luck. Perhaps the most striking gospel scene about seeking is the first disciples' encounter with Jesus by the Jordan when they were asked, "What are you looking for?" and Jesus then responded with the richly contemplative words "Come and see" (John 1:38, 39). But I am drawn more to a passage from Jeremiah to guide us as we elaborate the importance of seeking:

> For surely I know the plans I have for you, says the LORD, plans for your welfare and not for your harm, to give you a future with hope. Then when you call upon me and come and pray to me, I will hear you. When you search for me, you will find me; if you seek me with all your heart, I will let you find me, says the LORD. (Jer 29:11-14)

There is no need to rehearse the comments made above about the will of God; in this text "plans" would be tantamount to "aims" or "intentions." What is intriguing here is the way the prophet joins fervent searching—"with all your heart"—and discovery. The searching does not consist of an aimless, existential restlessness; it designates instead a focused, concentrated seeking after the mystery of God. In other words, seeking proceeds from faith. And the "finding" that ensues does not mean, equivalently, that all one's problems will be solved, all bad fortune will be reversed, or all losses will be restored. A person's fortune may indeed change, but deliverance from one's enemies or being healed of infirmity is not infallible confirmation that one has found God.

---

12. Augustine, *The Confessions*, trans. Henry Chadwick (New York: Oxford University Press, 1991) 3 [Book I(1)]. I omitted the scriptural references that Chadwick included in parentheses. The passage is interesting for the way Augustine underlines the importance of preaching in the awakening of faith—the ecclesial origins of the desire for God. Seeking God as desiring God (I do not believe these are exactly equivalent interior movements) is thematic throughout *The Confessions*.

A phrase frequently associated with Ignatian spirituality is "finding God in all things." The expression builds on a comment made by Jerónimo Nadal, one of Ignatius' trusted associates, that Ignatius was a "contemplative person even while in the midst of action."[13] Ignatius himself wrote in the Society's *Constitutions* that members of the Society "should often be exhorted to *seek* God our Lord in all things"[14] —wording that carries a different nuance. In the "Contemplation to Attain Divine Love," which he locates in the Fourth Week of the Exercises, that is, during the days devoted to meditations on the Easter narratives, Ignatius supposes in the retreatant a desire "for interior knowledge of all the great good I have received" in order that, moved by an awareness of blessing, the individual "may become able to love and serve his Divine Majesty in all things."[15] There follows a series of considerations about one's experience of divine goodness, a goodness richly manifested in oneself, the physical universe, and salvation history.[16] God "dwells," he notes, in everything from atoms and molecules to human beings, who are God's temple.

In one sense, then, these reflections tell us how Ignatius went about "finding" God in all things. He looked around and within, just as the psalmist centuries before him had contemplated the beauty and goodness of the universe as well as the mystery that is the human being itself.[17] But the grace Ignatius directs us to ask for in the "Contemplation" is that of *serving* God in all things, which I take to mean responding at every moment, in every situation and in everything that happens to us with a spirit

13. *Ignatius of Loyola: Spiritual Exercises and Selected Works*, ed. George E. Ganss (Mahwah, N.J.: Paulist Press, 1991) 44.

14. Ibid., 292. Emphasis added.

15. Ibid., 176.

16. Ignatius's approach here contrasts with Augustine's in Book X of *The Confessions* where Augustine asks, "But when I love you, what do I love?" The many created realities that have delighted Augustine keep pointing beyond themselves. "Yet there is a light I love, and a food, and a kind of embrace of my inner man, where my soul is floodlit by light which space cannot contain, where there is sound that time cannot seize, where there is a perfume which no breeze disperses, where there is a taste for food no amount of eating can lessen, and where there is a bond of union that no satiety can part. That is what I love when I love my God" [Book X(6)]. See Chadwick, 183. Augustine wants to go beyond the created world to its mysterious, loving Ground. Ignatius tends to keep his attention fixed on the created world both as sign of that love and as the historical arena where God's redemptive love is at work.

17. When I see your heavens, the work of your fingers,
        the moon and the stars that you set in place—
    What are humans that you are mindful of them,
        mere mortals that you care for them? (Ps 8:4-5, NAB)

of "profound gratitude." One serves God by loving God supremely and by loving others in God.

To talk about "serving" God is to stretch language. We can serve or minister to each other and in doing so glorify God, but God does not have needs and certainly not a need for human praise. Divine service, therefore, is essentially a way of talking about fulfilling God's commands or even participating as a minister of the gospel in the redemptive mission of Jesus.

The servant/serving idea should not be pressed too far. The "servant" of Second Isaiah is presented as the instrument by which God's saving designs are realized. Nevertheless, God does not pull strings in order to manipulate the course of human events any more than God actually hardened Pharaoh's heart. Cyrus, too, is presented as a divine instrument,[18] while in her song Mary spoke of mighty rulers being pulled down from their thrones.[19] But once again passages like these reflect a way of interpreting historical events which, though deeply religious, is not helpful for explaining historical process. Are all political leaders divine instruments, whether they realize it or not? Have the mighty ones of history traded places with the poor and defenseless—does justice triumph always or only occasionally? Did Israel as the wounded servant finally contribute to the healing of the many?[20]

The expressions of faith that we find in these and similar passages are perhaps not so much about finding as seeking God. They testify to an acute longing for God and an effort of faith to discover the divine mystery (and thus to uncover meaningfulness) even in the midst of suffering. God does not engineer history but God is certainly a part of it insofar as people of faith continue to search. The words of Isaiah

> Seek the LORD while he may be found,
>   call upon him while he is near.
>   (Isa 55:6)

highlight the life-or-death urgency of looking for God, since if we do not seek we shall not find. As a result, the holy mystery of God would then withdraw from the human world altogether.

In the end, seeking God should never be confused with looking for answers to why certain things happen to us or what inscrutable design might

18. Isa 45:1ff.
19. Luke 1:52.
20. Isa 53:5.

be guiding humanity to its destiny. Seeking God has to do with daily prayer; looking for answers has to do with theology. Seeking God yields no political or economic dividends: working for justice does, but the pursuit of God appears to be an end in itself. I do not find it helpful to think that God brings us into the circumstances in which we find ourselves or that God lifts us out of tough situations that we may have gotten ourselves into. But for those who seek God, God will be found "in" every situation as the empowering ground of love. Strange as it may first sound, the setting of our lives is not providential because God put us into it. Rather, the setting becomes providential in the measure that it leads to a deeper awareness of God's presence within it.

The more the accent falls on "seeking," the more we ought to think about the way in which human intention becomes "pure." What are the motives behind our actions that govern our decisions? What are the desires that shape the way we think or give form to our loyalties or tease our imaginations and fantasies? The asceticism of the gospel and Christian discipleship involves centering ourselves totally and unambiguously upon the kingdom of God—or as Jesus put it—"seeking" the kingdom alone.[21] Intention becomes pure insofar as it is single-hearted, not diffuse or compromised by the innumerable attractions that waylay our seeking. People will possess the "interior knowledge" that they have found God in the measure that they are seized by the "profound gratitude" of which Ignatius speaks. But finding God is not exactly the same thing as finding contentment in one's work or the strength to carry on in difficult times or even feeling the presence of Christ in the poor. Being moved with gratitude to God prepares the way for how we greet everything that might happen to us, for good or for ill; it is what led Paul to exclaim,

> For I am convinced that neither death nor life, nor angels, nor rulers, nor things present, nor things to come, nor powers, nor height, nor depth, nor anything else in all creation, will be able to separate us from the love of God in Christ Jesus our Lord. (Rom 8:38).

---

21. Luke 12:31. The NAB and RSV translate the verb as "seek." The REB has "set your minds on." The NRSV has "strive for."

Chapter 4

What Is Distinctive
_____ about the Christian Religious Experience?

The fact that our spiritual lives develop over time and can even be mapped in terms of stages or degrees of immersion into the mystery of God has been well known to spiritual directors for centuries. The classic "ways" of purgation, illumination, and union name stages of the elementary religious experience we ordinarily name "conversion." Saint Thomas asked whether it was helpful to distinguish three degrees of charity— the beginning *(incipiens),* the advanced *(proficiens),* and the perfect *(perfecta)*—since spiritual growth consists fundamentally in an increasing capacity to love God and one's neighbor.[1] In his manual *The Spiritual Life,* Adolphe Tanquerey wrote:

> We make use of the expression, the *three ways,* to conform to traditional usage. We must note however that it is not [a] question here of three *parallel* or *divergent* ways, but rather of three different *stages,* of *three marked degrees,* which souls who generously correspond to the divine grace traverse in the spiritual life. Each way in turn has many *degrees* which spiritual directors must take into account . . . Likewise, there are in the various *stages* many *forms* and *variations* dependent upon the character, the vocation, and the providential mission of each soul. But . . . we [may] reduce these degrees to three, accordingly as a soul *begins, advances* or reaches the *goal.*[2]

---

1. *Summa Theologiae,* IIa, IIae, question 24, article 9.
2. Adolphe Tanquerey, *The Spiritual Life: A Treatise on Ascetical and Mystical Theology,* trans. Herman Branderis (Westminster, Md.: The Newman Press, 1930) 297–98. Italics in the original. The formality of the language notwithstanding, Tanquerey has actually drawn attention to the contours of each individual's religious experience. A less schematic approach is given by Joseph de Guibert in *The Theology of the Spiritual Life,* trans. Paul Barrett (New York: Sheed and Ward, 1953) 258–91.

I am not sure whether the convention of three major "ways" subdivided in terms of "stages" is so helpful as the idea of "location." For location connotes place and space, and place contains a strong social component. "Ways" suggests the individual pursuit of holiness; "location" suggests where we are in relation to others. As the "other" changes, so do we and so too does the "place" in which our souls stand. The relation, in other words, undergoes a process of clarification and purification every bit as penetrating as what we associate with the first "way." Thus the experiences corresponding to each of the four Weeks of the Spiritual Exercises of Saint Ignatius might be said to designate a progressive series of "locations" primarily in relation to the Jesus of the Gospels. The idea of stages of growth should not imply that the path of each God-seeker is in every respect identical, for there are too many human variables to take into account. Yet whether one's view of direction tends to be that of accompanying others on their interior journey to God or that of assisting others in their discernment about how best to serve God, sensitivity to the ways of the Spirit grows in us as the months and years of our lives go by. Conversion is what happens when a person experiences God's love for the first time—and every time after that. But the experience will not be exactly the same in each instance because in the spiritual life there is no backing up or repeating; we never stand in exactly the same interior space twice.[3]

Some human experiences are obviously universal. Each of us is born and each of us dies, which means that cultural metaphors which draw on life and death, growth and diminishment, can frequently be appreciated outside the specific cultures and societies from which the metaphors sprang. So too with experiences of loss and grief, of defeat and suffering at the hands of one's enemies, of thanksgiving and wonder or astonishment because good things happen and because from time to time the earth startles us with its splendor and captivates our imaginations. If we then add experiences of transcendence, moments when we are pulled out of the thoughts and feelings of our private worlds to delight in something refreshingly wider—a concert or dramatic performance, being in a crowd at the mo-

3. Christianity is not alone in recognizing the fact of stages of spiritual growth. The Buddha taught that "there are very different kinds of people who are at different stages of spiritual development, and according to whether they are 'ordinary persons, learners, or adepts,' each one is to be instructed differently." See Kevin Trainor, ed., *Buddhism: The Illustrated Guide* (New York: Oxford University Press, 2001) 49. For the Islamic analogue of the Christian "ways," see Annemarie Schimmel, *Mystical Dimensions of Islam* (Chapel Hill, N.C.: The University of North Carolina Press, 1975) 98ff.

ment of political victory, athletic events, making music together, and so on—there gradually begins to appear that reservoir of experiences which each human being can relate to at some time or another.

In short, accompanying men and women who want to become increasingly God-centered—who want to fulfill the great commandment literally and love God with "all" their heart, mind, and strength[4]—would not be possible unless a pool of common experience existed. Theoretically, whenever the interior journey commences at the most basic level with a person's wanting to reflect on and cultivate her or his relatedness to God, there is no other formal requirement of the "friend in the Lord" than that she or he be a person with prudence, faith, and an attentive heart. Practically speaking, however, the spiritual life does not build on the general but on the specific, not on the universal but the particular. Because scientific thinking requires the possibility of generalizing, Aristotle said that there cannot be a "science" of the particular; yet in the matter of each person's relating to God we come pretty close to having exactly that. All of us have experience of family life, but the ways in which families function and their members relate to one another can differ widely from one society to another or even between families in the same society. All have experience of suffering, yet suffering might not assume the same form in every life. For this reason, using imagination we recreate or reconstruct the circumstances in which others find themselves and then insert ourselves into those reconstructions empathetically. Nevertheless, at the end of the day one has to concede that there is an irreducibility about experience which cannot be escaped. If our thumbs and retinas furnish any clues here, each of us is as distinctive inside as we are outside. Hearts identify us as distinctively as fingerprints and eyeprints, but with far greater effect.

Most of us acquire a measure of self-reflectiveness and manifest a greater degree of self-transcendence insofar as we develop intellectually, morally, affectively, psychologically, and interpersonally. But is this what is meant by having an interior life? If interior life refers to the quality of self-awareness, self-knowledge, intellectual curiosity, and interest in others on the basis of their drinking from the reservoir of common human experience, then such people enjoy an interior life even though God is never formally part of it. If by interior life we mean, however, the development

4. Deut 6:5.

of a conscious relationship with the God who fashions us with a naturalist's fondness for diversity, then obviously there are human beings for whom the interior life would be altogether foreign. In any event, I am not persuaded that people progress logically from an interiority that does not know God to one that does. Certainly, spiritual direction should not be working from such an assumption. As we have intimated already, many are content if their desire for wholeness is satisfied by techniques that foster mindfulness, centeredness, bodily harmony, inner peace, and so on—lots of helpful things, but which stop short of the mystery of God.[5]

The Gospel Narrative as Structuring and Shaping Experience

The basis of the distinctiveness of Christian religious experience is the resurrection, death, and life of Jesus of Nazareth. The order of these moments is important, for the starting point from which every New Testament writer proceeds is the raising of Jesus from the dead. Theologians have been alert to this methodologically important fact for a long time, but because for most people the story of Jesus starts with Luke's depiction of the vision of Zechariah, the father of John the Baptist,[6] and then moves into Jesus' public life, they tend to hear the Gospel backwards. And starting the story backwards creates all sorts of difficulties when, as we study Scripture carefully, the difference between history and faith becomes increasingly evident and conceptually troublesome. In what sense can the scene of Jesus' walking on the water be "true," for example, if at the same time it is historically implausible?[7] How could anyone have heard what Jesus prayed in Gethsemane if he was prostrate on the ground and some distance away from the disciples and they were reportedly asleep?[8]

The four gospel narratives presuppose two basic facts. First, each evangelist believed that Jesus was not among the dead but among the living for

---

5. See, for example, Robert C. Solomon, *Spirituality for the Skeptic: The Thoughtful Love of Life* (New York: Oxford University Press, 2002). His chapter "Spirituality as Cosmic Trust" explains the importance of having a foundational confidence in the universe—in the rationality or intelligibility of being—since the alternative would lead to chaos and despair. The human spirit, in other words, has to postulate the trustworthiness of the world because human beings cannot survive humanly without R. D. Laing's "ontological security" (45). But if someone is going to make an option for the trustworthiness of the world, why not opt for the existence of God?

6. Luke 1:5ff.

7. Mark 6:48-49.

8. Luke 22:41; Mark 14:35; Matt 26:39.

the simple reason that God had raised him. And second, each evangelist belonged to a community that had actually experienced the kind of life or new form of human existence we associate with Easter faith. Now, my question is, How does a person who has come to know God in and through Jesus talk about *this* God with someone who believes in God but has never heard about Jesus? Can a person come to know the God who raised Jesus from the dead without first experiencing Jesus?

It is important to be precise here. That the God of Israel should raise the dead is not in itself a revolutionary idea, but we are not talking about the dead in general.[9] We are talking about Jesus and about what happens to everything he did and said precisely because it was Jesus of Nazareth whom God determined to raise, not some other Jewish prophet. For a Christian, experiencing God and experiencing Jesus are inseparable yet identifiably distinct aspects of the same religious moment. The formulas that Paul loved to use linking God—the Father—and Jesus in the same breath derive from an experience of following Jesus even though he no longer walks the earth. However, while he no longer travels the Galilean countryside, neither can he be counted among the dead: Jesus lives in the somewhere of our faith, our imagination, our liturgy, our communities, our daily lives, and our world. Above all else, there is no Jesus to relate to apart from images drawn from the gospel story, for the story is what constantly and perennially renders Jesus concrete—as concrete as the story with its manifold possibilities for being told and retold will permit him to be.

The Gospel and the Uniqueness of the God of Israel

While the distinctiveness of Christian religious experience must be traced to Jesus, the gospel is not fundamentally about Jesus; it is about Israel's God. For as a consequence of the life, death, and raising of Jesus, the God of Israel was about to enter the world's religious stage as the sole legitimate claimant to the roles of creator and redeemer. The idea that God is personal, has a proper name, and thus can be addressed in prayer is so deeply embedded in our religious awareness that we may miss its significance and take it for granted. There is no innate religious sensibility in human beings that guarantees the personal nature of God, no tiny voice

---

9. Jesus clearly believed in the raising of the dead (see Mark 12:18ff.). In the Old Testament, see also Isa 26:19; Dan 12:2-3; 2 Macc 7:14; and the metaphorical use of this image in Ezek 37:12-14.

crying to God from the depths of our being that attests to God's being more than a life-force, an energy field, or a shapeless cosmic spirit. The personal nature of God belongs to its Jewish imprint. The grand narratives of the world's and humanity's creation and the deliverance of the Israelites from bondage further circumscribe the way we think of God; they furnish us the texts and images from which our own religious experience is framed and constructed.

The sustained critique of institutional religion that we find in the prophetic literature together with the unyielding social message of the prophetic voices portrays God as both transcending religious structures and passionately invested in the fortunes of the poor. By the time Jesus appears on the scene virtually everything we know about God and divine concerns has already been disclosed from within Israel's historical experience. Human beings are left pondering the mystery whose depths forever remain beyond the capacity of language to capture: the love that alone explains why God elects to create in the first place, that "comes down" from heaven to rescue slaves, constantly surges within history through the prophetic defense of the weakest and poorest among us, and patiently instructs human hearts by dispatching Wisdom to pitch its tent among humankind. To claim that the God of our tradition loves us is, of course, absolutely correct; but the arresting feature of the claim is that divine love should have manifested itself in those particular ways.

Christians cannot maintain, therefore, that during his brief ministry Jesus taught something about God that had not been known previously. He did not refine or improve upon the moral teaching of his tradition, and he did not add to the store of human insight into the spiritual life. He established no new rituals or devotions, although the pattern of his meal-taking and table fellowship would become the basis of the Church's eucharistic commemoration of Jesus. Even the phrases of the Lord's Prayer have firmly Jewish roots, while the fact that Jesus addressed God familiarly as father is thoroughly consistent with Jewish spirituality.[10] What Christians do maintain, however, is that there is quite a difference between knowing the God of Israel before meeting Jesus and knowing God afterwards—a difference that would have been discernible to the earliest disciples and to Paul.

10. On the limits of Jesus' "Abba experience" see my essay "The Interior Life of Jesus as the Life of the People of God," in Robert J. Wicks, ed., *Spirituality for Ministers*, vol. 2: *Perspectives for the 21st Century* (Mahwah, N.J.: Paulist Press, 2000) 399–402. Also, see Daniel J. Harrington, *The Gospel of Matthew*, Sacra Pagina Series, 1 (Collegeville, Minn.: The Liturgical Press, 1991) 82–106.

All of the first followers were faithful, devout Jews (it would be hard to imagine their being anything less than earnest, committed, and believing people). Some of the disciples—perhaps most—had likewise traveled to the Jordan. They had wanted to hear and meet John the Baptist, and after listening to his words stepped into the religiously and politically charged waters of the Jordan.[11] They celebrated the feasts of their liturgical year and gathered each Sabbath for prayer services with their family and neighbors. They would have recited the Shema prayer, blessed the God of their ancestors for the food on their tables, and been mindful of the poor. They were, in other words, women and men of faith long before they met Jesus. The figure of Paul as detailed by his letters and the Acts of the Apostles illustrates this point in striking fashion.

The fact that the evangelists often present Jesus upbraiding his disciples for their lack of faith is somewhat misleading. That the people reading or listening to the Gospel might have to be invited or urged to deeper faith is fairly likely; all of us need to become stronger in our attachment to the Jesus we believe to be Son of God. Thus there may have been a catechetical motive behind drawing a picture of the disciples as people "of little faith." That the first followers would have had to struggle to understand the nature of the kingdom of God as Jesus preached it or that like all believers they would have had to face the daily challenges life sets before us seems pretty evident from the gospel narratives. Yet they had sufficient faith—in God, not in Jesus[12]—to set aside everything in order to be a companion of Jesus in the first place: "Immediately he called them; and they left their father Zebedee in the boat with the hired men, and followed him" (Mark 1:20). And later, when the mission was well underway: "Peter began to say to him, 'Look, we have left everything and followed

11. I have in mind the closing chapters of Deuteronomy and the opening chapter of the book of Joshua. The land beyond the river Jordan was the land of promise—"the land flowing with milk and honey" (Deut 31:20)—into which Joshua was to lead the people of Israel. Having escaped centuries of bondage in Egypt and having wandered forty years in the wilderness, the people were finally to achieve freedom and security, territorial integrity, and thus full national identity. Hence the water of the Jordan was charged with history, politics, and faith. The fact that John's ministry was located around the Jordan is significant, and the symbolism of Jesus—the new Joshua—emerging from its waters did not escape those who pondered the meaning of his life and death. The Jordan evoked lots of memories. One can imagine that rulers like Herod would have been suspicious of any movements that built on those memories and drew inspiration and hope from them.

12. I think the precision is important. As Christians, that is, in light of Easter, we relate to Jesus as we would to God; we put our faith in the risen Lord. But the first followers were relating to Jesus as disciples to a teacher. At the beginning of the story theirs was not yet a paschal faith.

you'" (Mark 10:28). When Luke portrayed the disciples asking Jesus to teach them how to pray, he was not implying that they did not already know what words to say to God. They were looking, rather, for a signature prayer, just as John had bequeathed a prayer to his followers.[13] Finally, when asked which commandment was the greatest, Jesus promptly answered that it was to center one's heart, soul, mind, and strength on God completely and unconditionally—and to love one's neighbor.[14] Once again we see the moral, theological, and spiritual continuity between Jesus and Israel; there is nothing distinctive yet.

In his study of experience in the New Testament, James Dunn concluded that the first Christians found themselves inhabiting a religious experience which was functionally, if not structurally, trinitarian. Experiencing God in this way would have increasingly set the early Christians apart from the Synagogue. Dunn writes:

> It is evident from Paul that the first Christians soon became aware that they stood in a dual relationship—to God as Father, and to Jesus as Lord. This relationship and awareness of it was attributed by them to the Spirit (Rom. 8.15f.; I Cor. 12.3). That is to say, Christians became aware that they stood at the base of a *triangular relationship*—in the Spirit, in sonship to the Father, in service to the Lord. . . . To say that the first Christians 'experienced the Trinity' would be inaccurate; they experienced *Spirit,* who made them conscious of their dual relationship as men of Spirit. Trinitarian theology should always bear in mind this primacy of early Christian experience, and return to it rather than to old dogmas as the starting point for fresh definitions.[15]

The Christian religious experience on this basis is certainly distinctive. It is important to notice, for the sake of theological methodology, that the idea of Trinity does not come down "from above"; it arises "from below," that is, from within the actual experience of Jesus' earliest followers. Trinity, in other words, is a practical or existential belief, not a speculative one. Speculation about the inner nature of God comes only secondarily and it is necessarily circumscribed by what the New Testament writers tell us, directly or indirectly, about how the earliest Christian communities experienced God. More descriptive than explanatory, early trinitarian language

13. Luke 11:1ff.
14. Mark 12:28-33.
15. James D. G. Dunn, *Jesus and the Spirit* (Philadelphia: The Westminster Press, 1975) 326.

affirms that to know Jesus is to know God, to love Jesus is to love God, and to be loved by Jesus is to be loved by God. Some of the language sounds at times adoptionist, yet if we bracket our knowledge of the christological controversies of the fourth and fifth centuries as we read the New Testament, then the passages that sound as if Jesus had been adopted as God's son—in much the same way that God "adopted" Israel's kings in the Old Testament—do not seem so jarring to our creedal sensibilities.

Adoption language does not resolve or explain Jesus' relationship to God; it describes by way of metaphor how God had owned all that Jesus was and did. Even the Fourth Gospel, where the union between Jesus and God is deployed so prominently, had recourse to metaphor as it sought to grasp the relationship between Jesus and God.[16] That relationship is the key upon which our very salvation depends: "What has come into being in him was life, and the life was the light of all people" (John 1:4). Yet it is hard to talk about the nature of that relationship without employing descriptive, even sacramental language: "No one has ever seen God. It is God the only Son, who is close to the Father's heart, who has made him known" (John 1:18).

The Christian belief that we most associate with the Fourth Gospel surely has to be the incarnation: "And the Word became flesh and lived among us" (John 1:14).[17] While we might not be able to prove beyond a

16. Dunn has also written that the christology of the Fourth Gospel is, from the viewpoint of the evangelist, fully within the bounds of Jewish monotheism. "If Jesus was the incarnation of Logos-Wisdom, then Jesus was thereby understood as the self-expression of God, that of God which may be known by human creatures—*God* incarnate rather than the *Son* of God incarnate, if the Son is understood as other than the Logos-Wisdom of God. As Paul's wisdom christology could still be maintained alongside, and even in the same breath as the *Shema*, so with John's: *Jesus as God, in the sense that the Logos/Wisdom is God—that of God which may be manifested within the limits of human history and flesh.* And thus the Fourth Evangelist maintained its christology within a monotheistic framework. But not in the perspective of rabbinic Judaism." See *The Partings of the Ways between Christianity and Judaism and Their Significance for the Character of Christianity* (Philadelphia: Trinity Press International, 1991) 244–45. Italics in the original.

17. I have argued elsewhere that incarnation is theologically dependent upon the resurrection. The enfleshment of the Word includes much more than Jesus' conception; it embraces the whole of his life, up to an including his death and resurrection. The prologue of the Fourth Gospel is thus a reflection on the whole story, not just its beginning. Divine solidarity with the human condition is not so much a matter of biology and physiology as it is of sociology and history. The fact that Jesus ate and drank, for example, is less religiously significant than the fact that he ate and drank with "sinners." The fact that Jesus died is less significant than the fact that he died by crucifixion. And so on. Not only was divine solidarity revealed at Easter, but the resurrection spread that solidarity horizontally into history. Incarnation would serve no purpose unless it worked "for our salvation," and in order for it to work for our salvation the enfleshed Word had to become present to men and women of Galilee and beyond. See my *Jesus in Solidarity with His People* (Collegeville, Minn.: The Liturgical Press, 2000) 2–3, 6–7.

shadow of a doubt that the evangelist had Proverbs 8 in the back of his mind when he penned that verse, the literary fact is that the Fourth Gospel has Hebrew Bible written all over it.[18] The idea of God dwelling among the people was hardly a religious novelty,[19] and the related idea that the divine presence "tabernacles" among them lies at the core of Israel's sense of being God's chosen people,[20] indeed, God's very child.[21] If we are searching for what is distinctive about the Christian religious experience, then certainly our belief in the incarnation should rank high; but we ought not to forget that metaphors and images from the Hebrew Scriptures paved its way. The story of Jesus bears witness to divine solidarity with the world—a solidarity that has immeasurable relevance to us—although it has to be situated along a trajectory that dates back at least to Exodus: "I have observed the misery of my people who are in Egypt; I have heard their cry on account of their taskmasters. Indeed, I know their sufferings, *and I have come down to deliver them* from the Egyptians"(Exod 3:7-8). The italicized words rightly remind us of a clause from the Creed: "who for our sake and for the sake of our salvation came down from heaven."

The Paschal Paradox: Strength in Weakness

As we continue looking for distinguishing features of Christian religious experience, we should perhaps turn our attention to the risen Lord's words to Paul "for power is made perfect in weakness" (2 Cor 12:9). Paul's opponents faulted him for some unspecified physical weakness, for not being an impressive speaker, and for not being sufficiently charismatic. How then could Paul claim to have the Spirit? Dunn writes:

> Paul's response is memorable and of lasting importance. Divine power does not manifest itself by making the believer powerful, but as power in weakness; only so may it be recognized as divine power [2 Cor 4:7; 13:3f.]. Weakness does not hinder or prevent the manifestation of power; on the

18. See, for example, Raymond Brown, *The Gospel According to John I–XII* (New York: Doubleday & Co., 1966) 18–37.

19. "And [Moses] said to [the LORD], 'If your presence will not go, do not carry us up from here. For how shall it be known that I have found favor in your sight, I and your people, unless you go with us? In this way, we shall be distinct, I and your people, from every people on the face of the earth'" (Exod 33:16).

20. See, for example, Exod 25:8; Ezek 37:27; or Zech 2:10-11.

21. Exod 4:22-23; Hos 11:1.

contrary it is the necessary presupposition of power, the place wherein and the means whereby divine power is revealed on earth [2 Cor 12:9]. . . . [P]ower does not drive out weakness; on the contrary, it only comes to its full strength in and through weakness [2 Cor 12:9]. . . . [P]ower without weakness is destructive. . . .[22]

A major theme running through Paul's theology and spirituality is the striking contrast between God's way and human ways, divine foolishness and human wisdom, divine poverty and human riches, the new Adam and the old Adam, and so forth. Both Gentile intelligence and Israelite expectation had been offended by a crucified messiah, whom God had raised from the dead. The cross of Jesus had not only been a political scandal; it proved to be a theological scandal as well. The virtues associated with the cross— humility, service, poverty, self-emptying, obedience—are the mechanisms by means of which God reaches into history and transforms the human world. The divine logic revealed by the cross and resurrection turned human reasoning upside down; it ran absolutely counter to ordinary human intuition both on the part of the wider Hellenistic imperial culture in which Paul preached and on the part of the regional culture and religious background of first-century Pharisaic Judaism from which he came. Yet Paul found confirmation of that logic in his own experience. Thus he had concluded, "for when I am weak, then I am strong" (2 Cor 12:10).

The divine logic that Paul had experientially verified pervades the gospel narratives; it is clearly evident in the shape and content of Jesus' ministry. Jesus' instructions to his disciples about service, detachment, sharing, humility, poverty, debt forgiveness, compassion; and the everyday witness of Jesus in terms of the company he kept, the people he welcomed and embraced, the demons he confronted, the risks he took for the sake of the kingdom, and his tireless work of teaching, listening, and healing—all of this illumines not just a divine logic but above all a divine preference. One of the chief signs that the kingdom was at hand was the fact that through the presence and preaching of Jesus God had indeed brought good news to the poor.[23] The "weakness virtues" in themselves are not simply counter-intuitive; in some cases they could prove downright harmful, especially if they were to deflect our attention from the hard, messy struggle against social, economic, or political mechanisms of injustice, violence, and subjugation.

22. Dunn, *Jesus and the Spirit*, 329.
23. Luke 4:18; 7:22; Matt 11:5.

Now it is undeniably true that nonviolent resistance can be a forceful tool for bringing about social change, as Mahatma Ghandi demonstrated in the campaigns in which he was involved against racism in South Africa and British imperialism in India. Commenting on Matthew's Gospel, Benedict Viviano writes regarding the instruction "Do not resist an evil-doer" (Matt 5:39):

> Jesus teaches non-resistance to evil in the sense of avoiding physical violence or damages. This leaves open the possibility of psychological or moral resistance, "media fighting," exemplified by Mahatma Gandhi or Martin Luther King. The parallel in Rom 12:19-21, based on Prov 25:21-22, is important in showing that Jesus' teaching is a strategy for winning, not for passive resignation or indifference to evil. The goal is to shame the opponent into a change of heart. This presupposes the requisite dispositions in the opponent, which are not always present.[24]

Commenting on the further instruction "Love your enemies and pray for those who persecute you" (Matt 5:44), Viviano continues:

> This is not hopeless idealism but a wise strategy for overcoming the persecutor. The heroic stance of the martyr gives the persecutor a bad image and is hard for governments to control.[25]

Nevertheless, I do not believe that what Gandhi did constitutes an example of turning the other cheek as a strictly evangelical practice. Gandhi's active, nonviolent resistance cannot serve as a concrete illustration of Jesus' teaching in the Sermon on the Mount, as I shall try to explain.[26] Neither, for that matter, were the hunger strikes undertaken by, say, Irish dissidents in British prisons[27] or by four Bolivian women under the repressive government of Hugo Bánzer;[28] nor was the silent protest of the Mothers of the Plaza de Mayo, whose vigil in Buenos Aires sharpened

24. Benedict T. Viviano, "The Gospel According to Matthew," *The New Jerome Biblical Commentary*, ed. Raymond E. Brown and others (Englewood Cliffs, N.J.: Prentice Hall, 1990) 643.

25. Ibid., 644.

26. On "passive resistance" or *satyagraha*, see Mohandas K. Gandhi, *Autobiography: The Story of My Experiments with Truth*, trans. Mahadev Desai (New York: Dover Publications, Inc., 1983) 284–85, 314–17, 392–93, 396–97, 413–38.

27. See David Beresford, *Ten Men Dead: The Story of the 1981 Irish Hunger Strike* (New York: Atlantic Monthly Press, 1997); or Bobby Sands, *Bobby Sands: Writings from Prison* (Dublin: Mercier Press Limited, 2001).

28. Their story can be found in Philip McManus and Gerald Schlabach, eds. *Relentless Persistence: Nonviolent Action in Latin America* (Philadelphia: New Society Publishers, 1991) 48–62.

the conscience of a nation and contributed to the demise of the military dictatorship that had kidnapped and murdered their children.[29] For non-violence as an effective political strategy is hardly an invention of the gospel or derivative from the Christian religious experience. And non-violence as a religiously motivated strategy always has to contend with the cries for justice and vengeance found in the book of Psalms, as well as in the fierce apocalyptic imagery of the books of Daniel and Revelation. Besides, where can we locate wholesale confirmation of the truth of this strategy on the part of Christian communities? Where has it been consistently lived and practiced? One would be hard pressed to demonstrate that the Church throughout the centuries has been "one, holy, catholic, apostolic—and nonviolent."

What about Loving One's Enemies?

A thoroughgoing commitment to forgiveness, based on the gospel's instruction that we are to love our enemies[30] and show ourselves as merciful as God,[31] would most assuredly set us apart religiously. The only way to account for why someone would consistently embrace such a radical position would be to cite the teaching and example of Jesus—the idea being that if individuals want to find God by entering a faith relationship with Jesus, they will find themselves drawn to putting his teaching into practice. And the truthfulness of the teaching would be confirmed by experience: in forgiving enemies and loving them one "knows" God.

Love of enemies represents a faith option, not a moral imperative. Love of enemies becomes reasonable to the degree that people experience divine love and grasp love's power to effect the deepest change. I am of the view that we do not learn to love enemies by practicing forgiveness exercises. The habit of love—a love that includes even one's enemies—is a spiritual ideal that is simply beyond human reach unless individuals have experienced themselves as loved by God. That is why love of enemies has

---

29. See Matilde Mellibovsky, *Circle of Love Over Death: Testimonies of the Mothers of the Plaza de Mayo*, trans. Maria and Matthew Proser (Willimantic, Conn.: Curbstone Press, 1997); and *Relentless Persistence*, 79–99. See also, Argentina, Comisión Nacional sobre la Desaparición de Personas, *Nunca más: The Report of the Argentine Commission on the Disappeared* (New York: Farrar, Straus and Giroux, 1986).
30. Matt 5:44.
31. Luke 6:36.

to be seen as a radical expression of faith. One may never know for certain whether such love will make the least bit of difference; there is simply no guarantee that hardened hearts will let themselves be touched by such spiritual depth. Both Jesus and Stephen died without knowing whether their final prayer would have any effect on those who killed them. Gandhi, it is said, admired Jesus' teaching about non-violence but lamented the fact that so few of his followers had actually practiced it.[32]

I would counter, however, that the issue is not that far too often we have failed to implement a moral teaching, but that maybe too few of Jesus' followers have really experienced God's love. Divine love alone reveals in what way the teaching is reasonable and divine love alone makes that teaching attractive. In short, if love of enemies were to be put forward as a distinctive feature of the Christian religious experience, then we should have to look behind the teaching for its experiential ground. For a Christian, the grace that empowers him or her to embrace this spiritual ideal would be the discovery of the love of God in the risen Lord. Yet theological caution is still called for. To the extent that people of any religious tradition arrive at the conviction that the mystery of God is the mystery of love, then sooner or later, insofar as that mystery penetrates a person's soul, forgiveness and love of enemies will become a spiritual fact of life.[33] Love of enemies is quintessentially religious and that is why it figures so prominently in the gospel. Jesus was a believer, a deeply religious man; he "knew" God.

In considering what is distinctive about Christian religious experience, we have been calling attention to important aspects of a believer's rela-

---

32. Gandhi had enormous esteem for Tolstoy, who he claimed was "the greatest apostle of nonviolence that the present age has produced." See *All Men Are Brothers: Life and Thoughts of Mahatma Gandhi as Told In His Own Words*, compiled and edited by Krishna Kripalani (New York: Columbia University Press, 1969) 175. I think it would be fair to say if someone had approached Gandhi for spiritual direction, she or he would have realized very quickly that, for Gandhi, God and nonviolence were inseparable, that a sustained practice of nonviolence was the condition of the possibility of experiencing God. But it is not clear to me that nonviolence was so central to Jesus' message as Gandhi supposed.

33. Drawing on the work of Friedrich Heiler in order to clarify what is central to religion, Bernard Lonergan drew attention to seven characteristics of the world's high or major religions. Chief among those characteristics is love: love as the nature of God, the necessity of loving one's neighbor, and love as the superior spiritual way. For Lonergan, as for Rahner, love is the chief expression of human self-transcendence. The quest for authenticity leads one, sooner or later, to the mystery of love, whatever one's faith tradition. See Bernard Lonergan, *A Second Collection* (Philadelphia: The Westminster Press, 1974) 149–63.

tionship with God; at the same time we have been setting aside what appears to be common to religious experience as such. When I emphasize the spiritual continuity between Jesus and the scripture, tradition, and practice of Israel which shaped his religious sensibilities, for example, I do not mean to subtract anything from their abiding significance. Jesus himself pointed out that "every scribe who has been trained for the kingdom of heaven is like the master of a household who brings out of his treasure what is new and what is old" (Matt 13:52). His mission was not about displacing the Law and the prophets—the Hebrew Scriptures—but about intensifying what is taught and promised there.[34] It may also be worth repeating that common or universal features of religious experience can only manifest themselves in the concrete, everyday experience of believers who stand within particular religious traditions. To grasp the significance of that experience, one has to start, not at the level of the universal or general structures of religious existence but at the level of everyday life and thought, the specific paths that women and men are actually walking. Indeed, one needs to pay close attention to the rituals and devotions, to shrines and churches and temples, to the enactment of pilgrimages and the use of amulets, medals, and so forth, to art, music, and architecture—to the myriad ways in which human beings perform their faith.

In short, we do not just "pray"; we pray as Christians, as people whose thinking and imaginations have been indelibly imprinted with the story of Jesus. We do not simply assemble for worship; we form the Church. We do not merely practice good deeds or "random acts of kindness"; we look for and find the risen Jesus in other men and women. We do not merely learn how to cope with suffering; we view all human suffering against the background of the cross and resurrection. For the cross does not merely put a Christian spin on suffering, diminishment, and death by insisting that they serve a redemptive purpose (which they certainly do). The cross forces us to behold suffering and God at the very same time—not suffering first, then God; or God first, then suffering; but both simultaneously. Our souls do not chance upon the love of God in some shapeless, indistinct way; they are awakened to divine love in the narration and everyday enactment of the life, death, and resurrection of Jesus by Christian communities.

34. Matt 5:17-18.

If Jesus did not invent either spirituality or religious practice, then neither did the early Church. Yet both spirituality and religious practice were thoroughly integrated with the gospel story. For example, the institution of monasticism antedated its third and fourth-century expressions in Christian figures like Anthony, Pachomius, or Cassian. Practices such as fasting, making retreats, almsgiving, and meditation are found in each of the world's major religious traditions. Whether one gives alms solely from the motive of compassion or because God expects us to do so or because we believe that to assist the poor is to assist Jesus, the result is the same: the hungry are fed, the naked are clothed, the homeless are welcomed, the sick are visited. It makes little difference in whose name the good deed is performed.

A Clarification by Contrast

In his engaging essay "In Ten Thousand Places, in Every Blade of Grass," Francis Clooney relates how, while preparing to lead a retreat for a group of predominantly Hindu students in Kathmandu, he came across a story from the life of the Buddha which put him in mind of Luke 7:11-17. Because it is both so moving and so instructive, I include it here:

> Gotami was her family name, but because she was frail they called her Kisa (Frail) Gotami. She had been reborn Savatthi into a poverty-stricken house. When she grew up, she married and went to her husband's house. But it was only after she gave birth to a son that they treated her with respect.
>
> But just when the boy was old enough to play, he died. Sorrow sprang up within her, and she went from house to house looking for some medicine that would bring him back. But people laughed, saying, "Where can you find medicine for the dead?"
>
> Finally, a wise man told her, "Woman, if you wish medicine for your son, go to the possessor of the ten forces, the foremost individual in the world of humans and the world of the gods. He is the Buddha, and he dwells nearby. He alone will know the medicine."
>
> So she went to where the Buddha was staying. She stood before him and asked him for medicine. Seeing that she was ripe for conversion, he said to her, "Go, enter the city, make the rounds of the entire city, and in whatever house no one has ever died, from that house fetch tiny grains of mustard-seed."

"Very well, sir," she replied, and she went off delighted in heart to look for that seed.

But in each house she entered, she found that someone had died: in one, a son; in another, a mother in childbirth; in a third, a man killed in war.

When she had finished going through the city, she had found no house where death had not entered. She exclaimed, "In the entire city this alone is the way of things! This the Buddha, filled with compassion for the human race, must have seen!" Overcome with emotion, she went outside the city and carried her son to the burning ground. She said to him, "Dear little son, I thought that you alone had been overtaken by this thing which people call death. But you are not the only one death has overtaken. This is the universal law for all human beings."

Then she returned to where the Buddha was.

He asked her, "Gotami, did you get the mustard seed?"

She replied, "Forget the mustard seed! I understand now what is life and what is death; only give me a place of refuge!" And he taught her; and even as she stood there she became established in the fruit of conversion, and requested admission to the Order. He granted her permission, and she took refuge in the Order.

Juxtaposing the story of the widow of Nain alongside this tale from the life of the Buddha, Clooney reflects: "When I meet the grieving, the disconsolate, I still hope to be like Jesus who heals, like someone who announces his good news, yet I also wonder about becoming someone who can open up the larger, inescapable patterns of life and death in this modern world where miracles are so rare and mustard seeds so common."[35]

The stories present us with two quite different religious experiences. One is a story about enlightenment concerning the human condition—"the universal law for all human beings"—which leads to a kind of submission or resignation to that law, and the other is a story about protest—the refusal to believe that it is God's will that widowed mothers should lose their only child. Now the New Testament is no stranger to the notion of resignation in the face of suffering that cannot be avoided. The prayer of Jesus in the garden is probably the quintessential expression of submitting to the divine will: "My Father, if it is possible, let this cup pass from me; yet not what I want but what you want" (Matt 26:39). And a

---

35. Francis X. Clooney, "In Ten Thousand Places, in Every Blade of Grass: Uneventful but True Confessions about Finding God in India, and Here Too," *Studies in the Spirituality of Jesuits* 28:3 (1996) 12–13. The text of the Buddha legend appears on pages 11–12.

few moments later: "My Father, if this cannot pass unless I drink it, your will be done" (Matt 26:42).

The fact that these words might not have been those of Jesus but were probably formulated by early Christians who had surmised what Jesus' sentiments were as he prayed on the final night of his life does not make their meaning any less clear. Still, it is important to note that the mood or tone of Jesus' prayer is by no means passive. Doing what God wants is always something active: such had been the pattern of Jesus' life during the whole of his ministry. Although he prayed regularly, he did not take refuge in meditation or withdrawal from the everyday world of human concerns; no monastery, no forest retreat, no desert refuge provides the backdrop for Jesus' mission. Early in the gospel story he declares that those who do God's will are his family[36]; he did not say those who "submit" or "resign themselves" to God's will, but those who put it into practice.

Each and every human being has to come to terms with the fact that we have been created by God, and since we have been created, we cannot lay claim to ultimate control over our lives. Dependency, finitude, and limitation are existential realities; it is useless to deny them and foolish to conduct ourselves as if they were mere fictions. Jesus comprehended this truth as fully as we do, or as the Buddha had some five centuries before him—not to mention Job, the Psalmist, or the author of the book of Wisdom. Christians usually reckon with these fundamental human realities by seeing Jesus as subject to the same laws that govern our lives and then in a second move by joining our historical existence inwardly to his. Yet Jesus is not especially known for urging people to come to terms with suffering, diminishment, and the limitations that human nature imposes upon us.

This leads me to think, therefore, that Jesus' prayer in the garden was formulated by a writer or storyteller who had in mind Jesus' messianic mission. And insofar as it was the prayer of Israel's messiah as he was about to drain the cup of suffering, the prayer is not so much about acquiescence or resignation; it is about mission. In other words, the prayer in the garden does not set the pattern for the prayer we might utter in the face of inescapable suffering, even though we might borrow Jesus' words on some occasions to express to God our willingness to be led, blindly if

36. Mark 3:35.

need be, along the path on which we believe God has placed us. The Gethsemane prayer was uniquely Jesus'; it was not meant to illustrate the normative Christian disposition in the face of suffering or death. The disciple can be next to Jesus as he makes this prayer, but strictly speaking the prayer is not the disciple's to make.

Consider Paul. He was heartened when he sensed that somehow his sufferings "completed what was lacking" in the suffering of Jesus: "I am now rejoicing in my sufferings for your sake, and in my flesh I am completing what is lacking in Christ's afflictions for the sake of his body, that is, the church" (Col 1:24). There is no doubt that Paul took deep consolation from the suffering he endured for the sake of the gospel, for in this way his conviction that he was truly following Jesus was experientially confirmed. But the sentiment misunderstood could come uncomfortably close to suggesting that Paul had become a co-messiah. Jesus had not just partially fulfilled his mission or role, however; he had drained the cup entirely. Fellowship in the suffering of Jesus can be a significant, meaningful, and confirmatory aspect of discipleship, but the New Testament is pretty clear that Jesus does something for us that we cannot do for ourselves—a realization that comes across when Paul wrote, "And the life I now live in the flesh I live by faith in the Son of God, who loved me and gave himself for me" (Gal 2:20).[37]

Is there something distinctive about Christian religious experience beyond saying that a Jesus-centered faith—the gospel lens—determines everything we think and say about God? If Jesus is the "form" in and through which we know God, the answer is no; there is nothing more to be said. Simply put, "He is the image of the invisible God" (Col 1:15); the life, death, and resurrection of Jesus has imprinted itself on our experience of God indelibly. But insofar as Jesus himself experienced God in a particular way, the answer I think is yes; there is something more to say about the Christian experience.

I do not know how one could ever prove that during his life Jesus of Nazareth experienced or knew God in a way that nobody else did. The New Testament makes numerous theological claims about Jesus, but the

37. If I may put the matter in Ignatian terms, Gal 2:20 sounds very much like a First Week experience, while the experience underlying Col 1:24 seem to emerge from the Third Week. For Ignatius, knowing oneself to be a sinner yet loved by God is the prelude to all subsequent growth in discipleship. The "Four Weeks" of the Spiritual Exercises mark progressive stages of immersion into the gospel.

evangelists composed their accounts of his ministry in light of Easter, and the New Testament letter writers obviously did the same. Thus the words and actions of Jesus are embedded within the faith life of the early Church. Yet its Easter-inspired belief about Jesus' unique relationship with God, a belief that approaches consummate artistic expression in the Transfiguration story, does not preclude the possibility that others besides Jesus had experienced God so closely that they too would have addressed him as Father. The inner life of Jesus is simply not accessible to us. The inner life of the early communities which gave us the Gospels, however—their experience of the risen Jesus abiding among them and in their hearts and minds—is another matter altogether.[38]

What Jesus said to Peter—"Blessed are you, Simon son of Jonah! For flesh and blood has not revealed this to you, but my Father in heaven" (Matt 16:17)—could apply equally to every disciple. None of us could encounter the risen Jesus in any way or place unless God had first made such an encounter possible; such is the experience underlying the text "No one can come to me unless drawn by the Father who sent me" (John 6:44). The discovery of Jesus is always a revelatory moment, a moment in which God makes something known to us that touches our affections, urges us to more compassionate living, quickens our hope, sharpens our awareness of mystery, induces gratitude, reverence, and humility, and permits us to behold the world as if we were watching sunrise for the first time. I don't believe we would be guilty of overstating the Christian case by claiming that for the New Testament writers, while God is clearly the creator, the eminent divine characteristic is that God is the one who makes Jesus known: not simply that God has sent or given Jesus to us as savior, teacher, and model of holy living, but that almost by [Christian] definition God is the one who leads a person to recognize Jesus as the Son. "Son," of course, is a title with deep biblical roots; it points to function, not to identity. That is to say, we cannot get inside Jesus and figure out what his self-understanding was, but we can get inside believers and their communities—inside our own experience—and figure out in what way the presence of Jesus has transformed their minds, hearts, and imaginations. The full meaning of the title "Son" has to be gauged in terms of the transforming or redemptive effect that the presence of Jesus risen has on someone's life.

38. See my essay "Interior Life of Jesus," 396–417.

When Jesus asked his disciples "Who do people say that I am?" (Mark 8:27) and then, refining his inquiry, continued, "But who do you say that I am?" (8:29), the evangelist was hardly implying that Jesus did not know who he was or that he was facing a crisis of self-identity. The question was meant to help the disciples—actually, to prompt those reading or listening to the story—to clarify their understanding of Jesus. Or perhaps more to the point, to help the reader clarify her or his own relationship with the risen Lord. Through Jesus' two questions the gospel text may in effect be asking about the difference Jesus has made in our lives. "What are people now saying *about you?* Who do people think *you* are after so many months with me?" If we were to reformulate Jesus' questions this way, then the replies "You are the Messiah" (Mark 8:29) and "You are the Messiah, the Son of the living God" (Matt 16:16) would in effect be reporting to us what Jesus has subsequently become for his community, namely, their savior. Or to state the point a bit differently, Peter could just as well have answered (on behalf of reader and disciple alike), "People are now saying that we are friends and companions of Jesus of Nazareth." In terms of salvation, I would think, it is more important that disciples grasp how they have been changed as a result of walking with Jesus than that they know how to name or define his identity. What we are now is a consequence of who Jesus is.

What Can Be Learned from Two Images?

On the shelf alongside me I keep two images, pictures of which are included here. The first is a bronze statue of the Buddha which I acquired some twenty years ago in Kathmandu. The second is a terracotta crucifix by the Peruvian artist Edilberto Mérida, with its oversized hands and feet, sunken rib cage, and haunting, even distressing facial expression.

The Buddha's eyes are closed, though his face gives the impression that he looks downward and into the withinness of things. He sits absolutely still, serene, detached from all worldly concerns, transcending everything. Yet his elongated ears suggest a listening so compassionate and so keen that no sound escapes him: the sound of fire and water, of wind and air, of plants growing, animals breathing, and of mortals—their words, deeds and inmost thoughts. His left hand lies open while his right hand touches the earth, recalling the moment when in a series of quakes earth itself had

Siddhatta Gotama
The Enlightened One (the Buddha)
Image from Kathmandu, Nepal

witnessed to his enlightenment. The Buddha has transcended desire and suffering and out of compassion for mortals is prepared to teach them the path to Enlightenment. Glancing at that image has the immediate effect of calming my soul, no matter what the reason for my anxiety or concern at the moment may be. I don't have to sit cross-legged on the floor, shut my eyes, and arrange my hands so that the fingers of one hand point upward while the other hand lies open to receive. I need only look at the image.

The crucifix, by contrast, is anything but soothing to look at. The most striking feature about the figure of Jesus is that he does not seem like just one human being. Somehow the figure of Jesus crucified makes me think of an enormous procession of victims, as if five hundred long years of the indigenous Andean peoples—years of conquest and colonization, the destruction of cultures, the introduction of deadly infectious diseases, the deplorable silver and tin mines, years of the "open veins" of Latin America[39]—were on the cross, too. The artist has created a crucifix that is not just about Jesus. His pain is not the personal suffering and torture which brought about the redemption of the human race—Jesus' unique and unrepeatable contribution to the history of salvation—but the suffering endured by women and men too numerous to count, victims all, whose lives have been crushed, not by disease or accidental misfortune, but by forces of institutional corruption, an unequal distribution of resources, social exclusion, and the collusion of religious authorities with unsavory political regimes. It would be a gross oversimplification to say that Jesus viewed himself as having been sent to preach the need for personal moral reform and rededication to the individual pursuit of holiness. These are important but nonetheless general and perennial religious goals. Their advancement cannot be divorced from the particular historical context in which preachers, teachers, and prophets find themselves. In short, the Peruvian crucifix draws attention to a haunting solidarity with the suffering humanity of his time and place that Jesus had demonstrated both in his living and in his dying. He groans and collapses under an incomprehensibly ageless burden.

39. The phrase comes from Eduardo Galeano, *Las venas abiertas de América Latina*. ET: *Open Veins of Latin America: Five Centuries of the Pillage of a Continent*, trans. Cedric Belfrage (New York: Monthly Review Press, 1973).

The Christ of the Protest
Work of Edilberto Mérida
Cuzco, Peru

These two images—the Buddha transcending suffering in an enviably serene contemplation and Jesus nailed to the world in a cry that speaks at one and the same time of protest, abandonment, and surrender—have helped me sharpen what is distinctive about Christian religious experience.[40] Needless to say, the Christian spiritual tradition has a familiarity with prayer, contemplation, mysticism, and ascetical practice that is both immensely rich and wonderfully diverse. A person's relatedness to God can range from being totally and visibly Jesus-centered to being at the fringe in terms of any identifiable connection with the Jesus of the Gospels. In general, however, the more manifestly Jesus-centered one's way of relating to the mystery of God, the more we can describe the underlying experience as specifically Christian.

Perhaps the point of contrast, then, concerns whether we find God *in* the suffering or above and beyond it. On the Christian side, God is found within it. But the ease with which we state this belief is deceptive since it is less the suffering itself than its historical form that captures our attention. In no way does Christianity preach or represent a mysticism of suffering as if suffering were in any way desirable for its own sake. It is misleading to speak of Jesus' going to the cross willingly, out of love for sinful humanity, as if the cross were his divinely appointed destiny. I think the gospel story is both more attractive and more credible if we insist that Jesus did not want to die; he wanted to live. But he also wanted life for his people, and that demanded a choice on his part: pursue the mission and, like John before him, face the prophetic consequence, or abandon the mission and retire to a safe haven in the Galilean countryside.

It is much easier to speak about destiny, mission, and divine plan by hindsight. In fact, that is probably the only perspective from which we can discern pattern or providence. As events unfold, there is no telling

---

40. Thomas Merton wrote: "It would be a grave error to suppose that Buddhism and Christianity merely offer various *explanations* of suffering, or worse, justifications and mystifications built on this ineluctable fact. On the contrary both show that suffering remains inexplicable most of all for the man who attempts to explain it in order to evade it, or who thinks explanation itself is an escape. . . . Suffering, as both Christianity and Buddhism see, each in its own way, is part of our very ego-identity and empirical existence, and the only thing to do about it is to plunge right into the middle of contradiction and confusion in order to be transformed by what Zen calls the 'Great Death' and Christianity calls 'dying and rising with Christ'." See *Zen and the Birds of Appetite* (New York: New Directions, 1968) 51. Merton's point is well taken, but it is important to differentiate between the suffering that "ineluctably" attends the human condition and those particular historical forms of suffering that arise because of injustice.

what the outcome of our lives is going to be. We have no way of knowing whether divine aims will have been thwarted or realized as a result of the major and minor choices that shape our lives and through which we mutually shape each another's lives. After all, there would have been no point in preaching repentance and renewal if in the end human salvation were divinely guaranteed; we don't work for peace under the premise that war and mutual annihilation are absolutely impossible. Maps cannot be drawn without giving coordinates and the coordinates in terms of which one might map a human life lie ahead of us in the future.

Early Christian thinkers "mapped" Jesus' life using biblical coordinates and it seems reasonable to say that during his ministry Jesus read his own experience in light of the prophets and psalms. But the possibility that he might have interpreted his suffering in light of the suffering servant imagery of Second Isaiah, for example, would not mean that God had destined him from eternity to be the fulfillment of those ancient texts. For those ancient reflections were themselves efforts to understand or account for the inexplicable misfortune that had befallen God's people. How could they be a people especially chosen and loved by God and at the same time undergo the disgrace and calamity of exile and captivity, unless the secret purpose of God was at work? Somehow, those texts reasoned, the salvation of the many would depend upon the holiness of the few—the servant who was God's instrument of salvation for the nations.

Christianity does not advocate suffering; but it does attempt to account for it, and it certainly assists people when they are afflicted by inviting them to ponder how in Jesus the divine mystery has shared the human condition. But Christian faith operates from the belief, founded on the gospel story, that the evils and misfortunes which plague human beings and their communities do not reflect what God wants. On the contrary, once the will of God reigns on earth as in heaven, every demon will be expelled, the sick will be healed, and those languishing in any sort of prison will be set free. The ministry of Jesus was proleptic in this regard, anticipating on a small scale the sort of victory that lies ahead, not so much in the next life as in the present one. The fact that demons in countless forms still roam the world and invade human lives, and the fact that heavy suffering persists everywhere understandably make us wonder whether Jesus' words for John the Baptist bear any trace of realism for today, but we do not doubt that Jesus spoke them and that he truly believed the reign of God was at hand:

"Go and tell John what you have seen and heard: the blind receive their sight, the lame walk, the lepers are cleansed, the deaf hear, the dead are raised, the poor have the good news brought to them" (Luke 7:22).

Granted, we would surely want to adjust those ancient signifiers of divine promise being realized; modern medicine has advanced far beyond what was conceivable even to the most skilled physicians of Jesus'—or Isaiah's—day. In this regard we have achieved "naturally" what many in the ancient world looked for supernaturally. The modern equivalent of "For nothing will be impossible for God" (Luke 1:37) must be worked out. That is, we have yet to delineate the signifiers that today's world would recognize as indications of divine power at work in the human world. Still, we do so from the supposition that the way things are is not the way the Creator intends, and it is that difference which leads us to hear the divine protest against the prevailing state of human affairs in the teaching and actions of Jesus.

It happens all the time that individuals are drawn into one another's suffering, for sympathy and empathy are manifestations of our nature: bearing one another's burdens is a telling indication of our ensoulment. The suffering that comes to expression on the cross, however, goes far beyond sympathy or the pain that might ensue from helping others in distress. The cross represents the resistance that awaits those who speak the truth and put it into practice; it forces us to behold in Jesus humanity's martyred prophets, all the men and women of history who have poured themselves out for others by resisting forces of injustice and oppression. Jesus was not killed merely because some people disagreed with his teaching. He did not die because he would not retract either his teaching or his beliefs. Jesus was certainly not killed by human beings acting as puppets in a divinely scripted drama requiring the death of the innocent one as the price of human deliverance. Jesus died because he had aligned himself with his people in their longing for a new and definitive exodus, for an end to exile, wandering, and captivity, and for a homecoming that would endure—the historical fulfillment of Moses' vision on the eve of the Jordan crossing.[41] By doing so, Jesus showed how much he refused to accept the world as it is. To understand why Jesus died, we have only to look at the

41. See Deut 30–31. "Although you may view the land from a distance, you shall not enter it— the land that I am giving to the Israelites" (Deut 32:52). "From a distance," we realize, refers to time as much as to geography.

loyalties and commitments that got him into trouble. He showed us why the route to God has to pass directly through the everyday lives of people. While the cross serves as a Christian symbol of resistance to evil, it also represents all victims. After all, the death by crucifixion was hardly unique to Jesus; he stands in an endless line of human beings who have been killed unjustly. Some of history's "crucified ones" were no more than innocent bystanders; others, like Jesus, were outspoken critics of repressive regimes. They dared to name and confront demons by pulling away masks and drawing attention to the demons' social, political, economic, and religious forms. But the connection between *Jesus* and history's victims is a paschal connection; the connection was made possible because God raised Jesus from the dead. In other words, the cross as a sign of divine solidarity with those whose lives have been stolen by people who resort to violence in order to protect their privilege—the cross as re-presenting victims—originates with Easter. In raising him from the dead, we believe, God has "owned" the mission and death of Jesus. Approved Jesus? Yes, Easter certainly attests to divine approval. Revealed him as "Son"? Yes, Easter likewise points to the saving difference between Jesus and us: he is (among other expressions) the firstborn, as Paul would put it.[42]

Yet the point is not merely that the death of Jesus as victim is different because he is Jesus, God's Son. After all, the "reason" for the Word becoming flesh was by no means simply to prove that it could be done. The "reason" concerns our salvation, to echo the Creed's important phrase: it was "for our sake" *(propter nos homines)* and "for the sake of saving us" *(propter nostram salutem)* that the Lord Jesus Christ "came down from heaven." The path to that salvation—that basic coming to wholeness which completes our creation, redemption, and sanctification—is nothing less than our entering a lasting, effective solidarity with victims. The reason why divine solidarity with victims is such a central part of the Easter message is that without the resurrection we would never *encounter* God in and at the cross. That is, our engagement with the cross would not

42. "For those whom he foreknew he also predestined to be conformed to the image of his Son, in order that he might be the first-born among many brethren" (Rom 8:29; RSV). NRSV: "the first-born within a large family." REB: "the eldest among a large family of brothers." See also Col 1:15, "firstborn of all creation"; and 1:18, "firstborn of the dead" (also in Rev 1:5). The New Testament has multiple ways of imaging Jesus, but the title "firstborn" is helpful in connoting both similarity and difference. As with every image or title, one cannot press it too far by making it the exclusive reference point for understanding Jesus. But the point is clear: we are part of a single family, Jesus and us.

be an event of our salvation unless the cross had the power to pull us to be wherever God is. And where is God preeminently to be found? With victims. This point is absolutely essential to a theology of spiritual direction since it furnishes an important criterion for recognizing the action of the Spirit in a person's search for God.

"Where the Spirit of the Lord is," Paul wrote, "there is freedom" (2 Cor 3:17). To follow through with Paul's insight into Christian experience, the decisive measure of a person's growth in freedom, of the vitality and resonance of his or her faith, is the degree to which a person approximates— inside and outside, both in prayerful desire and in everyday living—the mystery of solidarity that has been sacramentalized in Jesus on the cross. There is always something profoundly, unspeakably liberating about being where the Lord is.

Chapter 5

Further Elements
of Christian Distinctiveness

That the gospel story shapes our imaginations and provides a way of looking at the world and interpreting our lives is indisputable. Spiritual directors observe this fact probably more than anyone else in the Church. Indeed, they anticipate the emergence and development of a gospel imagination in those looking for God, if it is not already there. Whenever people catch a connection between their experience and the gospel story, they may be having what Ignatius on occasion identified as a vision. Two examples from the *Autobiography* come to mind. In the first he describes what happened to him once on the way to Venice:

> While on the journey to Venice, he slept in doorways because of the guards against the plague. It happened once that when he got up in the morning he ran into a man who, with one look, fled in horror, presumably because he saw him so very pale. Traveling in this way, he came to Chioggia, and with some companions who had joined him, he learned that they would not be allowed to enter Venice. His companions decided to go to Padua to obtain a certificate of health there, so he set out with them. But he could not keep up for they went very fast, leaving him at nightfall in a large field.
>
> While he was there, Christ appeared to him in the manner in which he usually appeared to him, as we have mentioned above, and this brought him much comfort.[1]

Later in Jerusalem Ignatius recounts that after having visited the Mount of the Ascension, he could not recall the position of the footprint

1. See *Ignatius of Loyola: Spiritual Exercises and Selected Works*, ed. George E. Ganss (Mahwah, N.J.: Paulist Press, 1991) 85 (No. 41 in the Autobiography).

in the rock and so he decided to return to the Mount, incautiously, without a guide. The story reads:

> When it was learned in the monastery that he had gone like that without a guide, the friars took steps to find him. So as he was coming down from Mount Olivet he ran into a "belted" Christian who served in the monastery. He had a large staff and with a great show of annoyance made as if to strike him. When he came up to him he grabbed him tightly by the arm, and he readily let himself be led. The good man, however, never let him go. As he went along this way, held thus by the "belted" Christian, he felt great consolation from Our Lord, and it seemed to him that he saw Christ over him continually. This lasted all through in great abundance until he reached the monastery.[2]

On both of these occasions Ignatius found himself in a situation that evoked images of Jesus in the Gospels. In the first instance, when he found himself in an open field at night, left behind by his companions, the scene that may have been in the back of his awareness was that of Jesus abandoned in the garden by his disciples. In the second, when he was standing in the same place where Jesus had been seized by guards, he found himself being grabbed and led away—an experience which triggered a similar sort of visionary experience. When imagination consistently references the events, circumstances, and so forth of our lives back to Jesus in such ways, human experience acquires its distinctive Christian pattern.

What Sort of Love Is Distinctive?

As we continue to trace the narrative lines that determine the distinctive shape or form of Christian religious experience, we approach what is perhaps the most insistent feature of the New Testament message about God, namely, that God is love and that the cross brings this love to the fullest possible expression. "No one has greater love than this, to lay down one's life for one's friends" (John 15:13). Now the specifically Christian point here is not that God should be conceived as love, or that love not just of

---

2. Ibid., 88 (No. 48). The "belted" Christians were Syrians—"Christians of the Girdle"—who appear to have worn a distinctive cincture. See Joseph N. Tylenda's note on No. 48 in Ignatius of Loyola, *A Pilgrim's Journey: The Autobiography of Ignatius Loyola*, rev. ed. (San Francisco: Ignatius Press, 2001) 101.

friends but also of enemies reflects a triumph of grace, although these are very important indicators of authentic religious experience. I think the Christian point—a point that lies at the core of all our preaching, worship, and practice—is that the encounter with Jesus risen includes first and foremost the realization that we have been loved, personally, individually, and inexplicably. Divine love is inexplicable because sinfulness, inadequacy, and incompleteness have been all too familiar a part of our lives.

To pick up the narrative thread, the story of the human flight from God starts in Genesis at the moment when Adam and Eve tell God, in effect, that they are afraid of their Maker:

> They heard the sound of the LORD God walking in the garden at the time of the evening breeze, and the man and his wife hid themselves from the presence of the LORD God among the trees in the garden. But the LORD God called to the man, and said to him, "Where are you?" He said, "I heard the sound of you in the garden, and I was afraid, because I was naked; and I hid myself." (Gen 3:8-10)

From this point forward fear tragically weaves itself into the human story. Initially, "the man" is afraid of God's seeing him and he attempts to hide; but as centuries pass, human beings will no longer remember why or from whom they are hiding. They will be plagued by the "fear of death," to follow the author of the letter to the Hebrews.[3] Paul seems to be voicing a similar thought in Romans 8:15, where he speaks about not becoming "slaves again to fear"—perhaps a subtle allusion to Adam, the first son, who had become a slave to fear.[4]

In the end, the fear of death is a fear about one's own worthlessness and poverty, for if human eyes were to see us as we truly are, then they would turn away from the grotesque self underneath the masks and cover-ups behind which we've been hiding. There are women and men, of course, for whom lying and concealment are nearly second-nature; they may have lost all awareness of how much they have become slaves to the fear of death. Most of us stand somewhere in between such self-deception and the full freedom of God's children, but we owe whatever degree of freedom we do enjoy to our living in the company of Jesus.

---

3. Heb 2:14-15.

4. I first discussed this theme in "Adam in Hiding," *Spirituality Today* 38:3 (1986) 243–46. The image of the first human beings hiding from the God who made them is one of the most descriptive means I can think of for portraying the roots of our sense of alienation from life.

If the fear of death is most evident in the strategies and defenses we de-
ploy in order to conceal a profound uncertainty and insecurity about who
and what we are, then it may be that the fear of death actually amounts to
a fear of life. It is disconcerting when someone has more confidence in us
than we have in ourselves. As a consequence we may be tempted to take
cover by resisting or downright refusing such trust. Indeed, we all have
personal limits and ought to possess enough self-knowledge to be able to
recognize them. But each of us may be able to point to instances where
the prospect of fuller life or greater freedom was actually threatening. I
think, for example, of the story of the paralytic by the pool of five porti-
coes.[5] He never directly answered Jesus' question about whether he
wanted to get well. Instead, he fumbled an excuse for why, after thirty-
eight years, he had still been unsuccessful in making it down the steps and
into the water. We can imagine that a dismal but not altogether unwelcome routine had long since set in: he had his own tiny but familiar place,
his beggar's cup, a step from which he could survey the world, and apparently his basic needs had been met. What would he be required to do
once strength returned to his legs? Accustomed to his victim status, the
paralytic might understandably have been afraid of the consequences of
being healed, which would shed some light on why Jesus later warned
him: "See, you have been made well! Do not sin any more, so that nothing worse happens to you" (John 5:14).[6]

Fear of death, fear of life: in either case, human beings are running away
from the one who created them. And the Christian gloss on this sorry
predicament is that God refuses to let the "Adam" in us run, hide, or settle
for a freedom only partially realized. For this reason many gospel encoun-

5. John 5:1ff.
6. Years ago, Archbishop Alban Goodier approached this scene from a moving, though slightly
different angle: "On a mat behind a pillar, alone and derelict, as if even in that grim assembly he were
an outcast, lay a man, filthy and deformed, with a disease upon him that was only too well understood. He had been there a very long time, so long that there was not a visitor to the pool but knew
him; for thirty-eight years he had hobbled to his corner every morning, and had begged his alms
every day, and at evening had hobbled back again to his lonely hovel in the city. It had been a dreary
existence, a dull, grey thing without heart or interest or care, that could scarcely be called living; the
one hope that had kept him alive had been that one day he might take his turn at the water and be
cured. . . . The man had grown old in his corner; he had seen his fellow-sufferers pass away, a few to
the pool for a cure, many more to death. He had come to look on life with a fatalistic eye, a doom
with another to follow it. He would lie where he was till the end, whatever the end was to be; he was
nothing to anybody, nobody cared, and why he went on living he did not know." See his *The Public
Life of Our Lord Jesus Christ* (New York: P. J. Kenedy & Sons, 1931) 112.

ters with Jesus involve the note of forgiveness. Forgiveness runs deeply through the narrative of his ministry, not because up until Jesus the God of Israel was not revealed as merciful and compassionate—otherwise, how would we account for the institution of sin offerings and guilt offerings, prayers like Psalm 51, texts such as Isaiah 1:18 or Hosea 11, or John's practice of baptism?—but because forgiveness meant coming home once and for all (to borrow a point from N. T. Wright[7]), and forgiveness is a word that has to be heard from God directly. In a well-known scene Jesus' adversaries murmur within themselves that Jesus is blaspheming when he assures a paralyzed man of divine forgiveness. They reason to themselves that only God can forgive sins.[8] And they are right, although on grounds that may not be immediately apparent. The theological point is not that sin, being an offense against the divine majesty, can fittingly only be "forgiven" or made clean by God. Rather, the theological point is that forgiveness is a creative action. To forgive means to create anew and to breathe the divine spirit once more into the lifeless forms we have turned back into.[9] Since God alone can refashion or recreate the human heart, God alone can forgive sins.

Another major feature of the ancient Christian experience, therefore, was the overwhelming conviction that in and through Jesus God had refashioned hearts and minds. Such was their experience of being a "new creation,"[10] where new creation is another way of expressing how the reality of forgiveness feels. Encounters with Jesus risen typically though not exclusively were experiences of forgiveness and reconciliation, as the resurrection appearances make clear. But if we press the formula a bit we come to appreciate that forgiveness happens when human beings are finally able to hear that God's love is unfailing, that there is no need to run any longer, and that in fact their cover-ups and flight were basically misguided, fruitless attempts to move out of God's sight. The fear of death, like the fear of life, reflects a fear of God: and this fear represents the great screw-up that followed the serpent's deceit. In the presence of Jesus, men and women were hearing the voice and beholding the face of God—God assuring them, personally and individually, that they were immeasurably loved and incomprehensibly desirable.

7. See N. T. Wright, *Jesus and the Victory of God* (Minneapolis: Fortress Press, 1996) 268–74.
8. Mark 2:2-7.
9. Gen 2:7.
10. 2 Cor 5:17; Gal 6:15.

Yet this last feature would remain incompletely sketched if we failed to look beyond the experience of being a loved sinner to the realization that we belong to a loved race. As John 3:16 makes supremely clear, divine love embraces "the world." "World" refers not only to the sum of all the individuals who inhabit the planet and who are prone to self-centeredness, disobedience, isolation, and alienation, but also to the cosmic wound or fracture that we associate with original sin. Facing up to one's personal, individual sinfulness is one thing; staring at sin as the totally irrational flight from life and the disastrous fall into division, hatred, and violence involves a meditation on a vastly different scale. In Christian faith such a meditation normally starts with the cross.

The historical forces which brought Jesus to his death are in some figurative sense agents of dark powers whose tendrils run deep across the entire human scene: in our minds and memories, our relationships and institutions, our untamed desires and fantasies, our cultures and language. The meaning of the cross, however, goes beyond concentrating our attention on the proportions and horrible reach of evil. The cross brings together divine outreach and human refusal, divine creative intent and human presumption so forcefully that in the end we see no other way to face evil apart from the way God does. In short, the Christian religious experience never permits flight from the world; it does not concede any ground to those who would say that "the world" is too ugly to love. God does not love the world merely because by nature God *has to love* everything the divine hand has made. God loves the world, rather, because God beholds its inherent goodness. And loving the world means drawing it to the wholeness we call redemption. The world, we might say, is simultaneously crucifying and beloved.

Already and Not Yet: Eschatological Expectation

I am not enamored of the word "eschatology" or its adjectival form. Not only is the term fairly specialized and rather challenging to explain, but because Jesus' mission and message are so heavily—well, I suppose the word has to be used—"eschatological," readers of the Gospels may get the impression that there is something highly speculative and complicated to the story. The expression "already and not yet" sounds far more intelligible to nonacademic ears, both because the words have fewer syllables and because there is an already-and-not-yet character to much of ordinary human experience.[11]

As religious people all of us live from hope. To the degree that the hopes we have and share are even partially realized, our lives take on an already and not yet character. I am not referring to the "plans" that we have and share because plans tend to consist of realizable projects and goals that we have set for ourselves. These projects require perseverance and resources of various kinds, including the strength that comes from religious faith. But in principle they do not depend upon "outside" assistance: *we* can bring them to fruition, if we try hard enough. At any rate, hope is not the same thing as the confidence we exercise in formulating and working towards our goals. Hopes and goals are not exactly equivalent. Why? Because while it is certainly possible to achieve our goals, what we hope for will never be fully realized in this life.

Hope is one of the three theological virtues, one of the structural features of the human relationship with God. In the limiting case, therefore, the "object" of our hope—like the "object" of our faith and of our heart's longing—is the divine mystery itself. To the degree that any human being has a conscious relationship with God, that person's interior life will be marked by faith, hope, and love. But most of us do not walk around all day explicitly hoping for God. Instead, this virtue suffuses or pervades everything we do, everything we say or imagine, everything we set our hearts on. Hope defines the atmosphere in which our spirits are constantly breathing. Hope is a manifestation of God-centered lives. There is an incompleteness to human existence that we simply do not have the resources to remedy. Faith enables us to name that incompleteness and love is the only way to navigate through it; but hope understands that incompleteness is not going to be our final state. Incompleteness will not have the last word with respect either to our individual lives or to human history itself.

In his parables Jesus drew attention to the enormous contrast between humble beginnings and extraordinary finishes. The kingdom of God, he

11. See James Dunn, *Jesus and the Spirit* (Philadelphia, Penn.: The Westminster Press, 1975) 308–18. Also, Monika Hellwig, "Eschatology," in Francis Schüssler Fiorenza and John Galvin, eds., *Systematic Theology: Roman Catholic Perspectives* (Minneapolis: Fortress Press, 1991) 2:349-72. Eschatology is different from apocalyptic. On the apocalypticism of Jesus, see Bart D. Ehrman, *Jesus: Apocalyptic Prophet of the New Millennium* (New York: Oxford University Press, 1999). On the contemporary relevance of eschatological thinking, see John Polkinghorne and Michael Welker, eds., *The End of the World and the Ends of God: Science and Theology on Eschatology* (Harrisburg, Penn.: Trinity Press International, 2000).

said, is "like" many things of ordinary life—yeast, mustard seed, lost coins, and so on. The miracles and "mighty works" that were features of his ministry indicated a new reality in the making. The reign of God was about to break through. When it finally did, all demons would be chased out of hiding from human hearts, all lepers would be cleansed, all the blind would see, all the lame would walk, all withered arms would be made strong, all the deaf would hear, all prisoners would be set free. When the reign of God broke through, no peasants would be indebted to landowners, no family would be without its field, no individuals or groups would be forced to live at the margins of their communities, and widows would never again mourn the loss of their only child. Debts would be remitted, forgiveness and reconciliation would reign and even the dead would be restored to life. Such was the horizon of expectation within which Jesus spoke, healed, rebuked, preached, instructed, and invited people to discipleship. Was Jesus unbelievably unrealistic, or was he totally, unapologetically God-centered? Even granting that some of these signs of God's reign were figurative, the fact is that Jesus lived from hope and his imagination was decidedly eschatological. He beheld the immediate, everyday world in light of an inspired expectation of what was yet to come and that expectation was confirmed by events that occurred in his ministry.

The point where this kingdom expectation turned explicitly Christian, however, came *after* the resurrection. Some of Jesus' early followers concluded that the raising of Jesus marked the beginning of the end-time. What had happened to him, they figured, was soon to happen to everyone else. On this score they confused their experience of the risen Lord with their enthusiasm about his being alive and their eagerness to join him. It took time for them to realize that their mission of giving witness to him would be long-term, spanning generations and cultures. It took time to realize that God had raised Jesus not to announce the beginning of the departure of the righteous from the earth, but to reveal an abiding love and presence. The "ascension to glory" did not mean that Jesus was leaving his followers, but that he was staying.

For Christians, then, the "already and not yet" nature of our experience includes two elements. First, there is a difference between what we are and what we shall be, between the life of the Spirit that we presently enjoy and the fullness of that life which yet awaits us. Second, the believer knows Jesus to be truly present and yet at the same time really absent. Let me elaborate.

Each of us has a vision of what the Church should be, or Christian marriage, or religious life, or discipleship. Each one has an idea, more or less precise, of what "kingdom of God" refers to. Each of us intuitively senses, I think, that our definitive union with God will not have to wait until the last human being dies. We will not be languishing in graves until the great trumpet sounds. The fact that the Church does not embody the vision perfectly, or that we have not yet achieved a perfect marriage or a perfect following of Jesus or a perfect actualization of religious charisms; or the fact that humanity is far from living the unity and peace that the Creator intended, or that the "ideal" self is yet to appear in us—none of this should undermine our efforts to bring about what we long for. And the more we strive, the more we realize that human effort alone will not be enough because the desires or expectations that move us do not ultimately spring from us. Desires may be channeled through or shaped by the social reality which is the Church, but their energy still ultimately comes from God.

The "perfect" Church, as a living realization of Jesus' prayer—"May they all be one; as you, Father, are in me, and I in you, so also may they be in us"[12]—does not yet exist. As a result, the Catholic Church prays unceasingly for this to come about: "Grant that we, who are nourished by his body and blood, may be filled with his Holy Spirit, and become one body, one spirit in Christ."[13] Similarly, the perfect disciple does not exist. But the word "perfect," like the word "ideal," is tricky. "Ideal," especially when conceptually coupled with "perfect," suggests an impossibly high standard. Whenever we judge ourselves against that standard, we shall always fall short and are likely to succumb to chronic guilt. Perfect love of God is manifest not in the attainment of the highest possible spiritual state but in the constant, uneventful, everyday effort to lead a God-centered life. Since our actions seldom measure up to the gospel ideal as we've imagined it, I suspect that divine judgment about us gets weighted on the side of the richness and intensity of our desires rather than our deeds.

A major aspect of our experience of Jesus risen, then, is the sharp awareness of the difference between what we are and what we can yet become. Rather than inducing feelings of guilt or inadequacy, however, this awareness eats away at complacency and intensifies our desire for Christian wholeness. In knowing Jesus, we understand what we are capable of and

12. John 17:21 (REB).
13. The Third Eucharistic Prayer.

called to be, but the risen Lord's invitation to deeper life comes across as a consolation rather than a burden. We certainly do lament our sinfulness, but we do not experience sinfulness like those who have never found the risen Lord. People may experience severe moral inadequacy in the course of their lives and have to deal with it, but moral failings are generally not viewed under the category of sin unless a person belongs to a religion. Nevertheless, Christians do not pursue moral beauty for its own sake; ethical perfection by itself, however commendable, is not exactly what our hearts are set on. For one who knows Jesus, sinfulness is never experienced apart from hope; and the ground for this hope is the twofold conviction that, first, only God saves and, second, that the "perfection" or completion of the individual has as its context the perfection or completion of God's saving designs for the human race. A redemptive situation of the victory of some individuals and the perdition of the many would be theologically incomprehensible. Christians experience sinfulness—their own and that of the wider human family—with hope because they understand that the human project does not rest finally in human hands. Or to put it in Paul's terms, "but where sin increased, grace abounded all the more" (Rom 5:20). Whether married or single, religious or lay, we confess our failures as Jesus' disciples; yet the awareness of failure is itself a grace and this grace renews our hope. While we are conscious of not being "perfect," the not-yet character of our experience never cancels out the "already."

There is indeed a life beyond this one, but the prospect of an afterlife is not the main reason why Easter gives us hope. The Easter proclamation—"Christ has risen!"—enunciates a basic gospel fact and an equally basic gospel experience. Jesus is not among the dead but among the living, and his being among the living means that people meet him in a rich variety of places and contexts: in their minds and imaginations, in strangers and in close friends, in families and communities, in moments of great suffering and moments of great joy, in their reading of the Bible and in liturgical assemblies . . . the list seems virtually endless. No matter where it occurs, every encounter with Jesus risen assures us that the existence of each of us here and now as women and men of faith is not going to be without effect. The present historical moment in which the Spirit of Jesus is working subtly yet steadily among us opens fresh possibilities for those who will come after us even though our vision is necessarily limited. Like Moses, we cannot peer much beyond the Jordan. Yet to believe with all one's heart in the possibility of "a new heaven and a new earth" (Rev 21:1) is neither naïve nor romantic, no matter how desperate the circumstances of our lives and of our times.

The future comes as gift or as a promise realized; it does not come as a project or a plan which we have labored successfully to bring about. No matter how hard we work, we cannot make the reign of God happen. Coming to this liberating insight is a feature of the paschal experience. In meeting Jesus risen we come face to face with our own incompleteness. Yet the accent in this paschal experience does not fall on how unfinished our spirits feel; it falls on the peaceful confidence we have that God will fill up in us what is lacking. These are not words of lovely but empty consolation, comforting us because we realize how much good we have so far failed to achieve or how much sinfulness remains to be rooted out. We are a combination of achievement and desire, and human desire needs to be understood eschatologically. That is, the fulfillment of desiring—of good, holy, salutary desires—is beyond the range of what any of us can do. Only God "raises the dead" or does the impossible. Only God can complete or fill up in us what is "lacking."

The second element to consider is how Easter shapes Christian experience by making us attend to the difference between Jesus' presence and his absence. Presence and absence name the "already" and "not yet" aspects of Christian experience looked at from a different angle.[14]

While underlining the continuity between the Jesus of the public ministry and the cross with the Jesus who has been raised from the dead,[15] the gospel accounts also draw attention to a real discontinuity. Each of the Gospels, it would appear, has been composed by individuals who were not eyewitnesses to the events about which they write, and in that regard everything they put down was narrated from the perspective of Easter. The character of Jesus in each of the Gospels has not been drawn as if the evangelist at any point had bracketed his own faith relationship with the *risen* Jesus. Thus there exists a deep historical continuity between the faith of the contemporary follower of Jesus and the faith of the communities which gave us the four canonical Gospels. At the same time, the risen Jesus transcends the limitations of space and time that so obviously

---

14. See Donald Gray, "The Real Absence: A Note on the Eucharist," in Kevin Seasoltz, ed., *Living Bread, Saving Cup: Readings on the Eucharist* (Collegeville, Minn.: The Liturgical Press, 1982) 190–96.

15. Thus we read: "You are looking for *Jesus of Nazareth*, who was *crucified*. He has been *raised*; he is not here" (Mark 16:6).

circumscribed him during his ministry. The Easter apparitions reveal Jesus being mistaken for a ghost[16] or a gardener,[17] or assuming the guise of a stranger.[18] Imagination can have a field day with the Gospels as we place ourselves in the scenes and situations recounted in the narratives. But the Jesus to whom we relate through those imaginative insertions into grain fields, synagogues, lakesides, villages, homes, sycamore trees, and so on, is always the risen Jesus. And the more habitually we practice these imaginative exercises, the more our own surroundings get read and understood through a gospel lens. Christian imagination transfigures the world.

The gospel writers, we might say, were telling the story of an absent Jesus; he had truly died and was buried. At the same time, they were drawing on their experience of the risen Jesus to guide them as they wrote. Like Paul, many a Christian has longed to die and be with Christ,[19] but this understandable longing is rooted in something much different from the longing we have for someone we once knew and loved but who has moved or passed away. Longing to die and be with Jesus is not the same feeling as missing Jesus. Properly speaking, we do not "miss" Jesus, first because he abides among us, and secondly because we never had the chance to meet him before he died. Jesus is not "absent" from our lives like the loved one whose passing leaves a huge hole in our hearts. His absence thus corresponds to the not-yet aspect of our experience.

Yet even then, is it true to our experience to say that we are looking forward to meeting Jesus in the way, say, people might talk about wanting to meet other figures from the past about whom they have read or heard? Are we waiting to see whether any of the religious pictures or statues of Jesus that we have seen match what he actually looked like? I don't think so. The absence of Jesus is about the incompleteness of redemption, which is something we actually do feel. For so long as there are men and women who are hungry, without homelands, without recourse to justice, without freedom; so long as there are people who are poor or in any way oppressed; so long as there are victims, Christians will experience the "absence" of Jesus—not the absence of the historical figure Jesus of Nazareth, but the unfinished nature of human salvation. The text that comes to mind is Romans 8:22-23, where Paul envisions creation itself groaning in labor pains. The pain is intense,

16. Luke 24:37.
17. John 20:15.
18. Luke 24:13ff.; John 21:4ff.
19. Phil 1:21-24.

even excruciating; but on the other side of that pain lies new life. We feel Jesus' absence in the pain that so evidently afflicts countless human beings, but this is not an absence that leads to despair. I think, rather, of Martha's words, "Lord, if you had been here, my brother would not have died" (John 11:21). In the face of so many desperate situations, we may find ourselves continually praying her words, "Lord, if you had been here, these things would never have happened." These are the words of a prayer, and the situations of suffering that we witness preoccupy us precisely because we are people who pray. We address the Lord in this way because we know that even while we do not see him his love is no less real. Hence Martha's next words, "But even now I know that God will give you whatever you ask of him": situations may be desperate, but they can never rob us of our hope. Or to draw on another text, the risen Jesus may feel to us as if he sleeps during the storm, but he never leaves the boat. That conviction, born from prayerful encounters with human suffering, belongs to the Easter experience.

Conclusion

The lengthy reflection on the distinctiveness of Christian religious experience that began in the last chapter and has continued in the present one brings me to the following four points.

1. The Christian's experience of God is framed and constructed on the basis of images and narrative details which are furnished by the Gospels themselves. The experience is not first God, then Jesus, or first Jesus, then God. We don't start from a general experience or knowledge of God and then find ourselves drawn to Jesus. Neither do we start from a relationship with Jesus and then move to discovering God, however logical and developmental these processes might sound. God is embedded in the gospel story from the outset. One never encounters Jesus apart from the mystery of God for two reasons. First, the fact that God raised Jesus from the dead is threaded into the Gospel story from its opening verse. And second, whatever Jesus does within the story has to be referred back to the Spirit that descended upon him in the Jordan—or even at his conception, to follow Luke and Matthew.

Obviously I am not claiming that there is no religious experience outside of knowing Jesus, but I am stressing that the spiritual paths represented by the world's major religious traditions are as distinctive as apples and oranges. Gandhi made an ecumenically shrewd observation when he wrote:

> So we can only pray, if we are Hindus, that not a Christian should become a Hindu or a Christian should become a Moslem, nor should we even secretly pray that anyone should be converted, but our inmost prayer should be that a Hindu should be a better Hindu, a Moslem a better Moslem and a Christian a better Christian. . . . I broaden my Hinduism by loving other religions as my own.[20]

But he was mistaken when he went on to say:

> Religions are different roads converging to the same point. What does it matter that we take different roads so long as we reach the same goal? In reality there are as many religions as there are individuals.[21]

Likewise Thomas Merton was spiritually on target when he wrote:

> If I affirm myself as a Catholic merely by denying all that is Muslim, Jewish, Protestant, Hindu, Buddhist, etc., in the end I will find that there is not much left for me to affirm as a Catholic; and certainly no breath of the Spirit with which to affirm it.[22]

But to visualize the relationship of the major religious paths in terms of the spokes of a wheel joined at a common center misrepresents the way different paths both make us into distinct human beings and invite distinctive experiences of the divine.[23] Everything that rises does not necessarily converge.

---

20. See Louis Fischer, ed., *The Essential Gandhi: An Anthology of His Writings in His Life, Work and Ideas* (New York: Vintage Books, 1983) 212.

21. *All Men Are Brothers: Life and Thoughts of Mahatma Gandhi as Told In His Own Words*, compiled and edited by Krishna Kripalani (New York: Columbia University Press, 1969) 59. The tough theological effort involved in coordinating Christian claims about the uniqueness of salvation in Christ with the presence of God in other religions is not helped by saying that divine saving action finds its "highest historical density" in the Christ-event. See Jacques Dupuis, *Toward a Christian Theology of Religious Pluralism* (Maryknoll, N.Y.: Orbis Books, 1997) 316. Dupuis continues: "the action of the word of God is not constrained by its historically becoming human in Jesus Christ; nor is the Spirit's work in history limited to its outpouring upon the world by the risen and exalted Christ." Fair enough. But the neuralgic issue to be faced is not about a nondenominational salvation as the turning away from sin or the human being's union with God after death; it is about the concrete experience of finding God in everyday life. In order to face this issue, I suggest, we shall have to depend less upon speculative theology and more on spiritual direction. The talking point ought not to be what makes Christian claims "true" but what makes them distinctive.

22. Thomas Merton, *Conjectures of a Guilty Bystander* (Garden City, N.Y.: Doubleday, 1966) 128–29.

23. In *Working on God* (New York: Modern Library, 2000) Winifred Gallagher writes, "Thomas Merton once compared the great traditions to spokes on a wheel that all lead to the same hub" (165). But I have not been able to locate the place where Merton says that.

When explaining that the finally or fully integrated human being achieves "a state of transcultural maturity," however, Merton noted that "transcultural integration is eschatological."[24] He realized, in other words, that no one transcends the constraints of social and temporal location. The spiritually "ideal" human is necessarily an enfleshed human and not merely the embodiment of a Platonic form of holiness. In his essay "Contemplation and Dialogue" Merton explored how from within their contemplative experience monks and solitaries can reach across doctrinal differences. There is no reason to doubt, he argued, that "supernatural contemplation" is to be found in the other major religious traditions of the world. There are mystics who are not Christian.[25]

But, we need to ask, is all mysticism alike? What would we need to do in order to prove it is—what experiential platform would we have to be standing on? Either the mystics Merton envisioned have shed or abandoned the particularities of the paths that have brought them to union with the divine—in which case all paths become relative to the summit—or each union with God is distinct enough to warrant our speaking about "different Gods." While it seems theologically correct to say that human beings change but God does not, ordinarily in relationships when one pole changes, so does the other. Thus if we change, in some sense God must also—maybe not essentially, but certainly in the way our minds and hearts have constructed their sense of the divine mystery.

Another way of appreciating the relation between particular religious starting points and the endpoint of contemplative union with the mystery of God is, following Johann Baptist Metz, to consider the mystical/political dimension of the Christian experience. Christianity can surely be characterized as a prophetic religion—so too Judaism and Islam—for the obvious reason that Moses, Jesus, and Mohammad were known as "prophets." But for all sorts of cultural and historical reasons their prophetic styles were manifestly different. For anyone who has read the Hebrew Bible, "prophetic" signifies a deep investment in the life and fortunes of God's people, a burning awareness of the depth and tenacity of injustice in the human world, a willingness to confront that injustice in ways that are both hard-nosed and dangerous—and a sense of God that

24. See *Thomas Merton: Essential Writings*, selected by Christine M. Bochen (Maryknoll, N.Y.: Orbis Books, 2000) 165–66.

25. See Thomas Merton, *Mystics and Zen Masters* (New York: Dell Publishing Co., 1967) 202–14.

seems to be proportionate to the prophet's passion for justice. "Mystic" or "the mystical state," on the other hand, describes someone for whom the mystery of God has thoroughly penetrated heart, mind, and imagination. In itself this "state" is by no means exceptional—indeed, it is to be anticipated in those who are earnestly seeking God. If it should come loose from the prophetic (or Metz's "political") dimension of Christian experience, however, the mystical pole will tilt toward the pure, dehistoricized, apophatic form one associates with Neoplatonism. Mysticism among Christians retains its evangelical imprint the more it flows from insertion in the world and from a mindfulness of its crucified ones.[26]

When I imagine Jesus and his disciples, I do not "see" a Zen master and his students; I do not think of him as a spiritual expert or guide whom one might approach for instruction about advancing in the interior life. His asceticism does not appear to have followed the lead of the Pharisees or John the Baptist. His wisdom, so evident in the parables and sayings that have come down to us, appears to have originated in village life, not from within the Temple precincts or the remoteness of a desert monastery. In his religious experience, perhaps because he was a prophet, the life of God and the life of God's people ran together. Jesus' contemplative oneness with God correlated directly with his oneness with the people among whom he preached, taught, drove out demons, and worked miracles. Or to look at the matter slightly differently, the people around him—with all the political, social, cultural, and religious definition New Testament studies can give them—channeled Jesus' experience of God just as much as the natural beauty of the Galilean countryside or the psalms he chanted in the synagogue.

The path one takes, therefore, is hardly incidental to the picture and experience of God that emerges in the believer's heart and mind. As we noted earlier, it makes as much spiritual sense to insist that there is a particular God corresponding to each of the religious paths as to propose the existence of a single God to whom human beings draw near by a multiplicity of ascents. I am minded of Andrew Greeley's comment as he concluded his reflection on Catholic sensibilities:

26. See Johann Baptist Metz, *A Passion for God: The Mystical-Political Dimension of Christianity,* trans. J. Matthew Ashley (Mahwah, N.J.: Paulist Press, 1998); also James Matthew Ashley, *Interruptions: Mysticism, Politics, and Theology in the Work of Johann Baptist Metz* (Notre Dame: University of Notre Dame Press, 1998) 169–204. The "mystical-prophetic" formula I take from David Tracy's monograph *Dialogue with the Other: The Inter-Religious Dialogue* (Louvain and Grand Rapids: Peters Press and Wm. B. Eerdmans, 1990) 9–26 and 93–123.

I do not want to argue with anyone who is not Catholic. I certainly do not want to suggest that Catholicism is better than your religion, only that it seems to be different. Again, I have shown only that the null hypothesis that there is a distinctive Catholic imagination cannot be rejected—a modest enough claim.[27]

2. Being with Jesus invites solidarity with victims. There is, therefore, a particular Christian slant on suffering. Not all forms of suffering are alike. The historical form of suffering represented by the cross concerns prophetic protest and anyone who elects to follow a prophet needs to take this prospect into account. The cross as a religious symbol certainly brings God and suffering together on other levels and helps people to endure what cannot be escaped. Nevertheless, the cross's power as a religious symbol should not be allowed to eclipse the political and social circumstances of its historical origins.

3. While love is a central aspect of religious experience, there are several important shades of difference to consider. We expect religions to encourage and promote love and compassion as a moral response or ethical disposition. We ought also not to be surprised that religions should think of the divine mystery in terms of love itself or mercy itself. What the gospel throws into relief, however, is the human person's experience of being brought face to face with the creative, healing force of divine love. That love is both sustaining and forgiving; it reconciles and makes whole. As a lifelong process of spiritual growth conversion is thus inseparable from the experience of knowing oneself to be a loved sinner. For Christians, every encounter with the risen Jesus is necessarily accompanied by a greater measure of reconciliation, not just with God, but above all with the neighbor and with one's sisters and brothers. The freedom that comes from this experience must be continually celebrated and reclaimed.

But besides the Christian's encounter with Jesus in which the believer knows that he or she is a loved sinner, there is the believer's encounter with the world. And insofar as one knows the world as a person who has experienced God in Jesus, the believer apprehends the world as simultaneously sinful and loved, too. We ought not to underestimate the spiritual

27. Andrew Greeley, *The Catholic Imagination* (Berkeley: University of California Press, 2000) 184. I would forego his modesty and urge that the gospel does indeed shape the way we view the world precisely because it permanently affects the lineaments of imagination.

potential of this aspect of Christian religious experience. To know God is to share the divine attitude toward creation and to grasp the significance of a love that redeems.

4. Finally, Christian religious experience bears an eschatological imprint insofar as its origin is the raising of Jesus from the dead. We experience both ourselves and the world as unfinished, as works in progress, but always against the horizon of hope. I do not mean simply that without hope human history looks bleak—something which is true enough. Hope is not merely a film that we place across the world, like a transparency that re-colors what is harsh to the eye; it is not a soul-tranquilizer that makes it possible for us to cope with anxiety. Scandalous disparities between rich and poor nations persist, humanity's appetite for violence seems unrelenting, and the mind's agility when it comes to devising schemes of death remains truly frightening. Those who trace themselves daily with the sign of the crucified One cannot be charged with being naïve about the tightness of sin's grip. Nevertheless, they refuse to read the world's news or ponder its condition apart from the abiding presence of Jesus risen; hope has reconstructed the pathways by which their souls perceive and understand.

I do not pretend that the elements I have identified as distinctive exhaust the religious experience of those who follow Jesus, but I do think that any attempt to step outside of that experience would be as phenomenologically complicated as trying to step outside, say, of one's family life. "Stepping outside" involves a lot more than mental exercise. In some way it would amount to unmaking or "deconstructing" the human self. I cannot dissociate myself from my Christianness the same way I take off a jacket or a shirt, any more than I can conceptually remove myself from my family and think of myself apart from the social and cultural determinants that have figured into the kind of human being I am. The same constraint holds true, I presume, for all of us. I can think of the other sympathetically and do my utmost to view life from the eyes of the other, to "pass over" into the other's world. But to know the world as the other does I would have to be born all over again into her or his culture, family, and social place. But then, of course, I would no longer be me.

Chapter 6

The Incarnation
as a Starting Point for Spiritual Direction

In two engaging, perceptive essays which appeared over twenty-five years ago William Connolly and Philip Land addressed the issue (although not exactly in these terms) of whether a person earnestly looking for God would eventually be led to discover divine solidarity with the poor or whether such a discovery would first require an immersion in their social reality. Is there a dynamic at work in the Christian's spiritual life that ultimately draws a person to make a preferential option for the poor, or does that dynamic require an insertion among the poor to set the process in motion?[1]

In order to answer this question I tried to re-conceptualize it by asking whether human beings would attain compassion simply by cultivating their interior life or whether growth in compassion at some point would be impeded without contact with the "other" who suffers. Compassion comes to mind because more than any other virtue compassion seems to describe the mystery of God. A person fully ensouled is a person who has become thoroughly compassionate. Compassion represents (to draw on an older yet sturdy language) the triumph of grace over nature. Compas-

---

1. See William Connolly and Philip Land, "Jesuit Spiritualities and the Struggle for Social Justice," *Studies in the Spirituality of Jesuits* 9:4 (1977). Along the same vein, after explaining the necessity of keeping action and contemplation together if the struggle for justice is to bear fruit, Kenneth Leech framed the issue this way: "The linking of contemplation and action is one of the essential aims of spiritual guidance. But it is necessary to allow the turmoil and ferment of contemporary struggles to shake the spiritual patterns in which we are frequently imprisoned or protected. Authentic spiritual direction must include preparation for threats to spiritual security, for inner disturbances of spirit, for confrontations with new knowledge and new visions. A spirituality of liberation must be open to such dangers and risks: a closed spirituality must be a spirituality of oppression and ultimately of death. . . . Direction involves listening, exposure, nakedness of spirit before the storm and the fire." See *Soul Friend: The Practice of Christian Spirituality* (New York: Harper & Row, 1980) 32.

sion, it may be worth noting, is not the same as sympathy or empathy. One can sympathize with others without necessarily being compassionate. Sympathy develops because we are fellow sufferers; all of us have to endure pain, diminishment, disappointment and loss at some time or another. "For the fate of humans and the fate of animals is the same," writes Qoheleth; "as one dies, so dies the other. . . . All go to one place; all are from the dust, and all turn to dust again" (Eccl 3:19, 20). Each of us mourns the death of loved ones. Each of us knows sorrow and regret.

But compassion is connected with forgiveness and forgiveness depends upon two things: the readiness to let go of injuries and an awareness of one's own inner poverty and sinfulness. In this regard what the act of forgiving means for us and what it means for God are quite different. Human beings cannot disappoint God or hurt the divine feelings; the very idea that we have that sort of capacity would constitute the worst sort of presumption. In forgiving us God does not "let go" of hurts and injuries committed by us, nor does God merely forget our trespasses or pretend they never happened. To speak of divine forgiveness, therefore, is to talk about what God alone can do: God creates. And what God creates is the new heart—the new Adam or the new Eve. Thus the psalmist prays: "Create in me a clean heart, O God, and put a new and right spirit within me" (Ps 51:10). As I remarked earlier, Jesus' adversaries were on the right track when they wondered who but God could forgive sins.[2]

Divine compassion proceeds from love pure and simple. Human compassion, on the other hand, follows a different route. There is a kind of poverty that characterizes the human condition as such, namely, the existential poverty that attends us because we are finite, limited and destined to die. None of us "owns" her or his life. Life is measured to us and in the end it must be ceded back to God. In the most basic sense, all human beings are born, live, and die poor, although not all ponder and internalize this fundamental truth. Nevertheless, the virtue of compassion emerges from the realization that human beings are joined by their common poverty. We should not be at all surprised, therefore, that this shared poverty would play a leading role in the spirituality associated with each of the major religious traditions of the world.

2. Mark 2:7. There is a sense in which our forgiving others contributes to or "creates" wholeness both in them and in us. See, for example, Solomon Schimmel, *Wounds Not Healed By Time: The Power of Repentance and Forgiveness* (New York: Oxford University Press, 2002).

The experience of being existentially poor spills over into desire and intention. Our nature's poverty leaves us little choice but to work diligently at keeping our desires focused and our intentions pure. While we might not go so far as Gandhi in devising "experiments with truth" or so far as Ignatius Loyola in testing the depth of our trust in divine providence,[3] we still have to face the daily struggle of maintaining our inner freedom. Indeed, we may on occasion be dismayed by how much the human heart still needs redemption or how much of the inner self remains unexplored territory. But does a confrontation with existential poverty and personal sinfulness lead logically, necessarily to solidarity with the poor? I do not believe it does.

Fostering contemplative awareness and a sensitivity to the heart's longing for communion will eventually transform a person in the direction of compassion, although not in the way that God is compassionate, since human beings reach compassion by following the route of their existential poverty. Nevertheless, compassion and solidarity represent different spiritual states.[4] Realized solidarity—or, stated with a little more bite, the preferential option for the poor—is a quintessentially evangelical achievement. While I am not prepared to argue that it is a uniquely or exclusively Christian virtue, solidarity as the living embodiment of the option for the poor is certainly an integral feature of Christian discipleship. The more a person's experience of God is shaped by the gospel, the more the person is going to want to be with Jesus. And the more one wants to be with Jesus, the more one has to notice the company Jesus keeps.

Solidarity, it must be noted, is not about evangelical action, at least not right away. The corporal works of mercy, for example, have long been recognized as essential to Christian living. Followers of Jesus know they bear responsibilities towards the most vulnerable members of society, a knowledge firmly planted in the prophetic traditions of Israel. And the Church has during the course of its history undertaken innumerable projects of

3. Throughout the *Autobiography* Ignatius recounts how he was determined to learn that divine providence could be trusted, and a practice he adopted as he begged for alms was to give away whatever he absolutely did not require. God had to be his sole security—not alms or his family name or his Spanish connections or human companions. Ignatius thus experimented with poverty. In his autobiography, Gandhi described the "experiments" he designed to test his spiritual and mental limits with respect to continence and nonviolence.

4. I noted this difference in "Looking for the Sign of Jonah: God's Revealing Light Today," *The Way* 38:1 (1998) 17–18.

mercy and charity all over the world—projects that have drawn their inspiration from the teaching and example of Jesus. But solidarity has to do with both a "union of hearts and minds" and a politics of alignment; it is about loyalties and allegiances and cuts across class lines. Solidarity entails seeing the human world consistently from the perspective of those who are disenfranchised, impoverished, or for whatever reason prevented from standing upright as children of God. People lying at the bottom or at the margins of society do not have to think twice about what they want from God or what they would consider to be good news. For them the form salvation should take is evident, immediate, and concrete. Just think of the people who approached Jesus or were brought to him.

In the Gospels, Jesus contemplated the human scene from the perspective of poor widows. He defended followers whose hunger did not obey the Sabbath rest and led them into the grain fields to pluck (and to "steal"?) the kernels. He understood the terrible financial and social burdens that afflicted families and communities because of paralysis, withered arms, mental illness, or chronic unemployment. Solidarity certainly expresses itself in actions on behalf of human beings in grave need, but at the same time solidarity is a way of being human. For a Christian, one's humanness becomes increasingly transformed by the humanness of Jesus and his oneness with the poor—not just with those who are existentially poor (which includes all of us), but in particular with those who struggle every day to prevent their lives and their dignity from being shredded by economic and social powerlessness.

What I am describing, then, is the logic of the Christian narrative. Every one of us learns about the "poverty" into which Jesus was born through the Christmas story. No matter whether Luke may have exaggerated the physical circumstances. Impressed upon our minds and imaginations year after year is the cold, the absence of room in the inn, the presence of shepherds, the state terrorism of Herod, and so on. Yet those details from the infancy stories were created on the basis of the way in which the life of Jesus had actually unfolded—how he lived, whose company he kept, his prophetic teaching, the miracles he worked, the authorities he challenged, and how he died. While this text does not supply conclusive evidence that Paul was thinking along these lines, I find his words

> For you know the generous act of our Lord Jesus Christ, that though he was rich, yet for your sakes he became poor, so that by his poverty you might become rich (2 Cor 8:9)

to be very suggestive. If Paul meant simply that Jesus' becoming poor—taking upon himself "the destitution of a beggar"[5]—was a matter of his joining the human race in its existential poverty, then the incarnation would forfeit some of its scandalous energy. The revelatory power of the incarnation is minimized if the incarnation refers first and foremost to Jesus' sharing in the "limitations and weaknesses as well as the finitude of human life."[6] The phrase "and the Word became flesh" is empty of historical meaning—and thus of any intelligible religious content—unless we have listened to the complete story—uncut and unabridged—about the ministry, mission, death, and resurrection of Jesus. For it was not the "becoming flesh" as such but the particular historical, social, cultural, and religious "flesh" of Jesus of Nazareth that would constitute Christianity's distinctive religious form. In the measure that our scholarly or spiritual efforts to understand Jesus lose sight of the historical coordinates that locate Jesus in first-century Galilee, our picture of him becomes unorthodox.

The cross, not as a Christian religious symbol that mysteriously embraces every form of human suffering, but as the particular historical instrument by which political and religious powers conspired to destroy a Jewish prophet, is not directly about a poor person's life but a modest life that became poor.[7] Many (though obviously not all) of the people who would have comprised Jesus' social world led economically and socially depressed lives; starting with the Christmas stories, the gospel tradition seems drawn to associating Jesus with those lives. Evidently Paul's beloved Corinthians did not stand at the top of the social ladder: "Consider your own call, brothers and sisters: not many of you were wise by human standards, not many were powerful, not many were of noble birth. . . . God chose what is low and despised in the world, things that are not, to reduce to nothing things that are" (1 Cor 1:26, 28).[8] It would seem to me, then, that Paul's words in 2 Corinthians 8:9—"yet for your sakes he became poor"—envision the low social status of the Corinthian community, that

5. Jan Lambrecht, *Second Corinthians*, Sacra Pagina Series, 8 (Collegeville, Minn.: The Liturgical Press, 1999) 137.

6. Ibid., 137.

7. See John Meier, *A Marginal Jew: Rethinking the Historical Jesus*, vol. 1: *The Roots of the Problem and the Person* (New York: Doubleday, 1991) 350–52.

8. Richard Horsley remarks that Corinth may have been "the most status conscious city in the Roman Empire." The members of the Corinthian community hardly appear to have belonged to the aristocracy. See his *1 Corinthians*, Abingdon New Testament Commentaries (Nashville, Tenn.: Abingdon Press, 1998) 52.

is, they presuppose a material and not simply an existential poverty on Jesus' part. Jesus' "generous act" could then be viewed as his preferential option for the poor.

In short, the incarnation forces us to look at the specific details surrounding the life and ministry of Jesus before we begin contemplating the general or universal relevance of the holy mystery of God inserting itself into the human world and identifying with the human condition "as such." The point is a major one. There have been any number of efforts to discover a trinitarian resonance within the spiritual experience of non-Christian religions and even to locate in them incarnational sensitivities.[9] I think that the theory behind such efforts is that if God is indeed triune, then any revelatory experience should bear a trinitarian imprint, no matter how faint. But the only way such theorizing could proceed would be by sacrificing the Spirit: the Spirit would have to cease being the Spirit *of Jesus* and become the trans-cultural, trans-historical, and trans-religious breath or power of God. The Trinity, in other words, would become the great universal idea that potentially could draw the religions of the world together.

The incarnation is certainly about divine solidarity with the human condition in its moral and spiritual frailty. As we have already noted, Jesus' reception of John's baptism may be the most vivid gospel affirmation that Jesus stands among sinners, praying alongside them, longing for God's rule on earth. Yet solidarity hardly stops there at the Jordan. The rest of the story testifies to the steadiness and intensity of Jesus' "option" to let the people of God penetrate his soul and reveal to him where God is to be found. There is no route leading to God that bypasses God's people. The life of God and the life of God's people flow back and forth into each other. We might even go so far as to say that the history of communities of suffering is a major expression of the "economic" life of God—the scriptural record of the human encounter with the God of Israel. God elected to accompany Abraham's children and dwell in their midst long before Jesus appeared in Nazareth. In this sense Paul Griffiths' remark,

> There is a trivial sense in which Christian doctrine is unique and an equally
> trivial sense in which it is not. Its trivial uniqueness lies simply in its his-

---

9. See, for example, Gavin D'Costa, *The Meeting of Religions and the Trinity* (Maryknoll, N.Y.: Orbis Books, 2000); Raimundo Panikkar, *The Trinity and the Religious Experience of Man* (Maryknoll, N.Y.: Orbis Books, 1973); Gavid D'Costa, ed., *Christian Uniqueness Reconsidered: The Myth of a Pluralistic Theology of Religions* (Maryknoll, N.Y.: Orbis Books, 1990) 3–80.

torical particularity, a particularity shared by no other doctrinal system; but every doctrinal system is, by definition, unique in just this formal sense[10]

is not well stated. The "trivial" sense of "historical particularity" is precisely what supplies the imaginative richness and texture of the gospel narrative and Christian religious experience.

Incarnation as Starting Point

Let me now address the central concern of this chapter about whether the incarnation can be a starting point for spiritual direction. The Christian director believes that the incarnation belongs to the unfathomable mystery of God and is not merely a Christian spin upon divine self-disclosure. Those seeking direction might not possess the least inkling of this aspect of the divine nature. But if directors are going to accompany men and women who are looking for God, then they have to acknowledge that the divine quest orients people in a particular direction. Religious experience may exhibit countless variations and religious expression may assume enormous diversity, but I would not infer from this fact that we should concede the existence of multiple divine "persons." Christian theology confesses that the divine mystery consists of three Persons, not hundreds, thousands, or millions. The quest for God necessarily moves in the direction of salvation if in fact human life is always life-in-relation to the mystery of God. One's spiritual growth, therefore, is necessarily a growth in relation to the God who creates, redeems, and makes holy.

For a Christian, however, the God who creates, redeems, and makes holy has assumed a history in human time. And the spiritual director, conscious of this fact of faith, needs to know where divine solidarity is likely to take or lead those who are looking for God. At the same time, it would be naive to think that people will be led by the Spirit along that path without guidance, without the mediation of social realities like communities of faith, tradition, sacred writings, preaching, liturgical celebrations, and particular moral practice. There may be a myriad of stars, yet the one that led the Magi took them to Bethlehem, not to Benares or Bodh-Gaya. A person might indeed be attracted to any number of the

---

10. Paul Griffiths, "The Uniqueness of Christian Doctrine Defended," in Gavin D'Costa, ed., *Christian Uniqueness Reconsidered*, 168.

world's holy sites, but the light of the Magi's star leads to the city of David. God-seekers might land upon the divine mystery through a process of trial and error, but rarely do they arrive there by accident.

I am not phrasing things this way out of an ecumenical insensitivity to Hinduism, Buddhism, or any other religious tradition but out of an attempt to take seriously the religious place from which the Christian director begins listening to others. For I do not see how we would be able to throw our own Christian experience of God into phenomenological brackets—suspend the specifically Christian determinants of our experience—without doing a disservice to the gospel and the Eucharistic community. To be sure, innumerable human beings believe in God without putting their faith in Jesus; this point is indisputable. And their faith "makes them whole," that is, it will ultimately bring them into union with God. This point, too, is unarguable. Furthermore, I do not see that any long-term theological gain will come from trying to figure out how, in some secret, invisible, mysterious way, their saving union with God is essentially tied up with Christ. That, of course, is what Karl Rahner attempted to do with his theory about "anonymous Christianity,"[11] an effort that is readily comprehensible to anyone who has pondered, say, the opening chapter of the letter to the Ephesians. But the writer of Ephesians is describing the new, saving universe of Christian experience, not composing a Christian metaphysics.

Rather than talking about the truth of doctrinal propositions, I believe we should be talking about distinctiveness; rather than pressing metaphysical claims, we should be sharing experiences of salvation. Soul-friends may listen to us, question us and thereby help us to clarify elements of our own history of looking for God. But a spiritual director also guides us and, speaking from his or her own experiments with prayer and grace, the director implicitly gestures toward Jesus. The God I know—and the only God I know—is the God who has been revealed in the life, death, and resurrection of Jesus of Nazareth. I also realize that many other people have a different experience of God—not accidentally

11. Rahner's idea of anonymous Christianity served to bridge the Christian claim that God had reconciled the world to the divine self through Christ and the overwhelming evidence that human beings could be deeply religious without ever knowing Jesus. He had to argue, therefore, that the transcendence toward which human beings were oriented was intrinsically christological. The argument may have soothed some Christian apologists and dogmaticians but it has not been helpful for promoting inter-religious dialogue. See "Anonymous Christians," *Theological Investigations* 6 (London: Darton, Longman & Todd, 1969) 390–98; "Christianity and the Non-Christian Religions," *Theological Investigations* 5 (London: Darton, Longman & Todd, 1966) 115–34.

different but substantially different, at least if the words, symbols, and actions that carry their experience mean anything.

We all have parents, but all parents are not the same. What makes us distinctive and interesting is the particular parents we have been given, the particular family configuration we have been born into. Although we regularly use the word "God" as a form of address in our prayers, "God" is less a proper name than a title, a role, or even a job description. "Father of our Lord Jesus Christ" and "Yahweh": these are proper names, and with the naming comes both a history and an identity. What makes us distinctive is not that we believe in God but that we believe in the God of Jesus.

Now, I do not want to begin wading in metaphysical waters—although it may be that a swim in metaphysics will prove inescapable for a fully theological understanding of the process of spiritual direction. But it seems to me that our idea of God cannot be larger than the image of God that determines how we live and pray. Language obviously has its limits, as anyone who has ever tried to express his or her deepest feelings has had to admit. Theologians remind us often that the mystery of God exceeds the capacity of human language and of the mind itself and thus they have recourse to unrestricted "desire" as a way of naming the mind's orientation towards the unfathomable mystery of God. But shall we settle for identifying God with the experience of transcendence? Does that identification not run the risk of turning God into an abstraction or an idea? Ideas do not exist except in our minds, which means that "God" would not exist except as a construction of human intellects—God as the "cause" or "reason" for the world's existence. But "the God of Abraham, Isaac, and Jacob," "the LORD, the God of Israel" exists—both in our minds and in reality. The "God and Father of our Lord Jesus Christ" exists, again in human minds and in fact. And the Christian evidence supporting this claim comes from the particular experience of salvation that followers of Jesus continue to describe and testify to.

Perhaps the divine mystery should not be conceived as lying at the end of the process of desiring, striving, praying, and loving—the incomprehensible horizon that awaits us. The holy mystery of God, with its excess of presence over the images and words used to name that presence, lies, rather, within the concrete, immediate experience of salvation.[12] For this

---

12. On the idea of the "hypergivenness" or "saturated" character of the present [experience of salvation] see John D. Caputo, "Apostles of the Impossible: On God and the Gift in Derrida and Marion," in John D. Caputo and Michael J. Scanlon, eds., *God, the Gift, and Postmodernism* (Bloomington, Ind.: Indiana University Press, 1999) 185–222.

reason, "and the Word became flesh" has to be an incontrovertible pre-supposition for the Christian who engages in the practice of spiritual direction. The divine mystery in its fullness is already located in the present encounter with "the God and Father of our Lord Jesus Christ," however inchoate or undeveloped that encounter may be, however much time its unfolding will take. The human search for God is likely to leave us hopelessly disoriented and adrift unless, with a nod to Karl Barth, God is simultaneously looking for us.[13]

In an aside he made about the difference between the Gospels of Mark and Luke, David Tracy characterized Mark as a "fragmentary discontinuous non-closure, apocalyptic gospel grounded in fragments of the memory of suffering." Luke/Acts, on the other hand, reflects a "view of history as fundamentally structured like a continuous realistic narrative."[14] While I want to avoid too sharp a contrast, it occurs to me that the "God" of Luke/Acts is the God of the end of time, drawing all historical events in inscrutable fashion towards their ultimate consummation. Luke's is God of the whole, a totalizing God, the one true creator God who constitutes the destiny of the human race. Mark, however, does not share this sort of totalizing vision. One notes this absence both in the way the Markan narrative reads, with its abruptness, its interruptions, its fragmentary character, its stress on conflict, and its alignment of Jesus with those who have been poor, humiliated, rejected, and eliminated (a characteristic that we also find, of course, in Luke). Mark prefaces his passion narrative with an apocalyptic reading of human history and he closes his Gospel with the scene that ever afterwards will challenge our perceptions of reality itself—the empty tomb. The narrative concludes on the note of fear, the evangelist's message still ringing in our ears: "you are looking for Jesus of Nazareth, who was crucified. He has been raised; he is not here" (Mark 16:6). The link between looking for God and finding Jesus is the cross—provided that we have learned how to behold on the cross all the crucified ones of Israel's history and beyond.[15]

13. "The God of the NT is a God to whom many may say Thou, as to a personal being. This Thou of man to God, however, is the response to God's Thou to man." See the entry under "*theos*" in Gerhard Kittel, ed., *Theological Dictionary of the New Testament*, trans. Geoffrey Bromiley (Grand Rapids, Mich.: Wm B. Eerdmans Publishing Co., 1965) 3:111.

14. David Tracy, "Fragments: The Spiritual Situation of Our Times," in *God, the Gift, and Postmodernism*, 178.

15. As Mary Catherine Hilkert writes: "If Jesus Christ is the one in whom we recognize the face of God, the image of God is to be found in the crucified peoples of today." See "*Imago Dei*: Does the Symbol Have a Future," *The Santa Clara Lectures* vol. 8:3 (April 14, 2002) 11.

A Prayerful Caution

The preferential option for the poor and solidarity with victims, I have been suggesting, are permanent features of the gospel way. In some respects this point has been memorialized best in the story of the rich man who wanted to know from Jesus what more he had to do in order to gain everlasting life. The sincere man was perhaps prepared to do nearly anything Jesus might propose, even conceivably to giving away his share of the family estate, but he could not lay aside his family name, his family's connections and influence, and the honor that went with such privilege, in order to join the faceless, nameless, socially insignificant class that had gathered around Jesus.[16] The gospel way is not for everybody; many will choose not to walk it. Or as Jesus cautioned, it would be better not to start building the tower than to leave the structure only half-finished.[17]

Following *this* Jesus, the one who draws people like us into uncomfortable social worlds, generally proves profoundly energizing. But this energy can take two forms, one positive and the other negative. Positively, a Christian discovers a freedom, a purposefulness, a oneness with others, and even a spirit of inexplicable blessedness and hope that comes from an unfailing mindfulness of victims. One worries less about herself or himself and becomes increasingly absorbed by what others are undergoing. The circle of prayerful concern grows wider and one's affective engagement with others becomes steadier, every trace of superficiality seems to disappear, and the

---

16. See Mark 10:17-22. For further comment see Bruce J. Malina and Richard L. Rohrbaugh, *Social Science Commentary on the Synoptic Gospels* (Minneapolis, Minn.: Fortress Press, 1992) 243–45. According to Matt 19:20 the man is "young." Mark may have imagined him to be young as well, even though he does not say so explicitly. Running up to Jesus sounds like something a young person would do. He has kept the commandments, he tells Jesus confidently, since he was a child—which does not mean that he is an old man at this point. Later in the Gospel two young men appear, one in the garden (14:51) and the other at the tomb (16:5). Following Bas van Iersel, it is tempting to see a connection here. Perhaps the evangelist has inserted himself into the story at these two points, once as someone who out of fear let go of his baptismal commitment and "ran off naked," and then later as someone who has returned and become a witness to the risen Jesus. The evangelist himself may have identified with the struggling disciples at many points. If so, then a process of literary assimilation may be at work when readers tend to picture the rich man of 10:17 as young. Since the evangelist portrays him sympathetically ["Jesus, looking at him, loved him" (10:21)], one has to wonder whether the evangelist might not have identified with the man as someone who had initially found the price of discipleship too high but who would never forget the experience of being loved. Perhaps the man's sincerity and goodness eventually won out and he rejoined Jesus "on the way"—at least in the evangelist's (and the reader's) imagination. The narrator, in other words, is probably not an old man. On the appearnce of the narrator within the story, see Bas M. F. van Iersel, *Mark: A Reader-Response Commentary*, trans. W. H. Bisscheroux (Sheffield: Sheffield Academic Press, 1998) 494–504.

17. Luke 14:28-30.

world itself feels closer and even worth dying for. And the reason? Because one is truly in the presence of the crucified and risen Jesus. The negative energy, however, consists of mounting anger and outrage, a sense of moral superiority, of having a "cause" upon which to spend one's life, and of resentment toward those who do not share the same conviction or who have refused to enlist in the struggle for justice. Negative energy leads to frustration and despair. One grows more resigned to the world's present state, quoting out of context Jesus' words "For you always have the poor with you" (Mark 14:7). In the end, we lower our expectations of God and conclude that the master of the house will never return.

In the preceding remarks I have been presuming that the spiritual director comes from a position of some social and religious privilege. We enjoy knowledge and skills, familiarity with the ways of the Spirit, a network of associates and companions in faith, a "place" in the wider cultural and social world that most would consider to be the acceptable mainstream. But let us turn the situation around and imagine two other possibilities. First, what might happen if someone were to approach us for spiritual help who is more like Bartimaeus than the rich man? And second, what might happen to us if we were to approach a person from the social world of blind beggars for assistance in finding the Lord or cultivating our prayer life?

In the first case we would be forced to confront a host of hermeneutical issues. In fact, I don't think we could be of much help unless we have had some degree of insertion into the social and cultural reality of poor people. In my experience, while they are indeed looking for God in their lives, the poor are far less likely to seek the help of a spiritual director and more likely to depend upon others in the same community for mutual guidance and support. This in itself might be an ecclesiological datum worth examining. At the same time, they tend to draw considerable strength from various forms of popular devotion and religiosity—as well as from Scripture—but one wonders.

Popular piety can provide a powerful means of coping with the hardness of life, yet at the same time it can cripple or suffocate spiritual growth. Excessive devotion to the passion and death of Jesus, for example, is unhealthy because usually its converse is the notion that God is somehow placated by suffering and sacrifice.[18] If God is not going to liberate them from their af-

---

18. For an interesting and engaging study of this cult of suffering, see Robert Orsi, "'Mildred, Is It Fun to Be a Cripple?': The Culture of Suffering in Mid-Twentieth Century American Catholicism," in

fliction, then perhaps the solution to their search is to identify God with their affliction. In which case, a spiritual director who understands the constraints under which the poor live can be of considerable help—and should be prepared to face a different brand of resistance, namely, the consolation of suffering. I never imagine Jesus in the role of a spiritual director in our sense of the term, but I believe his mission among Galilean peasants had to include enabling them to understand that in no way had God decreed their lot in life. Furthermore, Jesus would have spoken to them credibly, with the authority that came from solidarity. The piety, the asceticism, the prayerfulness, and the ideal of holiness he represented really were "new wine."

And thus we come to the second case, which in a number of ways would be analogous to the gospel story's rich man (or woman) approaching the poor Jesus for advice in drawing closer to the kingdom of God. In the story the man wants to know what must be done in order to "inherit" salvation—after all, he had already inherited a great deal of what this world could reasonably offer. What becomes clear is that Jesus has a far better grasp of the social and spiritual situation from which the rich man comes than the latter has of Jesus and the social place in which Jesus' feet are planted. Granted that the story is being told by an evangelist who believes Jesus to be the Son of God and that it is being heard by people who share the same faith (and thus we know something the man does not), nevertheless, the man shows enough religious desire to approach Jesus, even if Jesus declines the compliment: "No one is good but God alone" (Mark 10:18). But in the end camels do not slip through needles' eyes; the man leaves, one assumes, terribly distressed—not because of what Jesus had said but because of his own inability to alter his social station, even if that inability should cost him being with God in an exhilaratingly new way.

Whether or not a spiritual director can be of help to someone who is poor is contingent upon making the preferential option, as I have attempted to explain. The world of the poor must be neither romanticized nor refused. To romanticize that harsh human reality would be both foolish and counter-productive, but to resist stepping into it would mean rejecting "the way" Jesus walks. There are, of course, other paths to salvation—but then one never really gets to meet and to know Jesus, and one's inner self would be, I believe, sadly different for having missed that chance.

Thomas J. Ferraro, ed., *Catholic Lives, Contemporary America* (Durham, N.C.: Duke University Press, 1997) 19–64.

Can the poor who walk with God "direct" those of us who are privileged? Well, perhaps in some sense they have been doing so for a long time—through the Psalms, through the prophets, and through one of their own. If the Word has truly taken flesh within their social reality, then the poor very much have something to teach us about compassion and divine solidarity.

Chapter 7

Should Christian Spirituality
Move beyond Jesus?

The public ministry of Jesus lasted a relatively brief time, perhaps as few as eighteen months but probably not quite reaching three years. His ministry overall fits the profile of teacher and prophet, for while he certainly healed people, the healing miracles were kingdom signs, that is, they helped to illuminate his message that the reign of God was breaking upon the world. As I remarked earlier, it is hard to think of Jesus as a guru, although in the Fourth Gospel he is certainly portrayed as someone who engages in the "conversational word of God" in the encounters with Nicodemus and the woman of Samaria in chapters 3 and 4, and maybe even during his exchange with Martha in chapter 11. It may be tempting to wonder what sort of spiritual insight and religious wisdom Jesus would have developed and shared if he had survived into old age, but I doubt that the outcome of such an exercise would be all that satisfying.

The gospel tradition notes Jesus' prayerfulness at a number of points, of course, and readers realize that in addition to weekly synagogue attendance and periodic pilgrimages to the Temple, he would have prayed at the appointed moments of each day. The picture that emerges is one of a devout man steeped in the religious tradition of his people. Indeed, even his contemplative oneness with God rings with a certain ordinariness, for when asked what the greatest commandment was he immediately cited the words of Deuteronomy 6:4-5. Jesus, we have to suppose, observed that commandment perfectly, the very same commandment (or invitation) that everybody else in Israel had been given and was expected to follow. Yet at the place where his heart and God's joined, there was also room for the people, and thus Jesus drew attention to a "second" commandment, quoting the words of Leviticus 19:18. The scribe recognized at once the correctness of Jesus' answer (Mark 12:32-34). Oneness with God through love summed up the only way to holiness—an everyday holiness that would become visible in the sheer ordinariness of the way we love our neighbor. Jesus thus inherited a spirituality that owed much to the prophetic pattern of experience that we associate with figures like Isaiah and Jeremiah, to be sure; but Jewish spirituality covered all of life—witness the Psalms—and had Jesus lived longer there is no reason not to think that he would have found God in sickness and old age in much the same way that everybody else did. In short, as we have observed several times already, Jesus did not invent a religion and probably should not even be thought of as a spiritual founder the way, say, we think of Benedict or Bernard, Francis or Ignatius. Jesus preached and testified to the reign of God. It would be more accurate to say that after the resurrection he himself became a distinctive spiritual path rather than that he had generated a new spiritual path during his ministry.

Jesus and the Ever Greater God

There is a sound theological reason why it is important to situate Jesus within the faith and spirituality of Israel's religious tradition and to emphasize the fact that he was in every respect a believer. Each human life, including the life of Jesus, is in God's hands. God stands at the beginning and the end as the source of life and the final destiny both of individuals and humanity as such. In the gospel story the divine voice addresses the reader as Jesus begins his ministry. It is heard a second time at the Transfiguration and at the end it is God who raises Jesus from the dead. At its deepest structural level the gospel story is about what God does as the unseen actor in history. Jesus' vision of his mission was fairly circumscribed. He apparently spent the greater portion of his time in the towns and villages of the Galilean countryside, seeking out the "lost sheep of the house of Israel" (Matt 10:6). But God's aims were far more ambitious; the God of Israel, after all, was also God of the nations: "I am the LORD, and there is no other" (Isa 45:5). The daring missionary outreach to the Gentiles would come later, with Pentecost. God, we might say, had designs on the life of Jesus that far exceeded anything Jesus would have been able to foresee. Maybe Luke had this wider theological plan in mind when he wrote, "Therefore let the entire house of Israel know with certainty that God has made him both Lord and Messiah, this Jesus whom you crucified" (Acts 2:36).

Yet a similar observation could be applied to any human life or even to moments in the life of the Church. We work, we pray, and we strive to live in union with the mystery of God; but none of us will be around when human history is harvested.[1] However discerning, far-reaching, and bold our vision, human eyes can penetrate just so far, and we certainly cannot fix the course of future events. In short, we have no way of knowing the ultimate impact our lives will have upon the spiritual climate of the world and we have no way of assessing the scope of God's creative engagement with us. When it comes to the future, historical causality and randomness have to play together. What God can draw from an event like the Second Vatican Council, for example, goes far beyond the daring yet necessarily limited and finite perspective of the bishops who participated in the conciliar deliberations.

But to return to Jesus: the fact that Jesus did not elaborate, say, a theology of suffering or bequeath a treatise on prayer should hardly trouble us. Luke's insight into the fact that the same Spirit that overshadowed Mary and later came upon Jesus at the Jordan had also descended upon the Jerusalem community confirms the point we are making. Development is bound to occur because we exist in a dynamic relationship with our physical surroundings, our culture, other women and men, and with God. In the course of developing a spirituality all its own, the Church has reached into the wider human community for practical insight and spiritual wisdom; we usually call that process inculturation. And whatever insight, practices, or wisdom it appropriated, the Church did so in terms of the Spirit of the risen Jesus. The Church did not merely import; it also reshaped.

Gospel spirituality derives its primary features from the pattern of Jesus' life, and that life, as many biblical scholars have noted, took on a decidedly prophetic character. In this regard, the death of Jesus and the death of John are thematically linked—John imprisoned and beheaded by Herod for speaking and behaving like Elijah, Jesus arrested and crucified by the Romans for speaking and behaving with the boldness of Jeremiah. While the parallels to those classical prophets might not be historically smooth, the fact remains that any spirituality modeled after Jesus will have to bear the stamp of protest and resistance. And it will heavily accent service.

The older we get, however, the more our physical freedom and emotional energy are likely to diminish. At the same time, our capacity for solidarity

1. Mark 4:29.

and forgiveness increases. Recourse to prayer may become more frequent and the actual praying more fervent. The realization of how much we share in humanity's original fracture becomes more penetrating. Our expectations of God grow both more confident and more desperate, for we know that we cannot redeem or remake the world, no matter how much in our youthful evangelical enthusiasm we may have presumed otherwise. How then do the followers of Jesus age or mature in the Spirit without relinquishing their prophetic moorings and aspirations to be of service? How do they "imitate" Jesus at those points where he left them no instructions or example? In the end, do apostles "retire" and become hermits? Do prophets withdraw to desert caves or mountain recesses, there to finish out their days in quiet surrender and observe the world from afar?

It is not enough to propose that the passage of years is supposed to bring out the more contemplative side of our nature. Action and contemplation ought not to be juxtaposed—neither early in life when physically we feel strong nor later when energies wane. Each stage of life does indeed prompt an appropriate, distinctive form of prayer as our relationship with God deepens and grows more familiar. But the relationship between action and contemplation, like the axis mystic/prophetic, is really one of simultaneity. The fact that physical capacity diminishes should not impede the force or scope of one's prophetic experience of God. For what is at stake is the way we share in the divine passion for justice, not the range of our moral or political energy. What proves increasingly decisive for the sort of person we want to be is our solidarity with others, our readiness to turn outwards rather than gravitate inwards, to become more world-oriented even as our mobility and practical effectiveness decline. One feels more yet does less, one shares more of the divine pathos even as one drifts to the apostolic sidelines.

Jesus of Nazareth, needless to say, did not pass through this later stage of the interior life, for his ministry ended abruptly and his final words (following Mark and Matthew) resound with the feeling of a work or mission left terribly unfinished: "My God, my God, why have you forsaken me?" (Mark 15:34; Matt 27:46). Granted, Luke adjusted those sentiments with protestations of resignation and surrender,[2] with declarations of pardon and forgiveness.[3] Nevertheless, Jesus died the way many of us will, namely,

---

2. Luke 23:46. Though uttered in the garden, the words of Mark 14:36 would hardly have been spiritually out of place at the cross; but they would have interrupted the narrative flow.
3. Luke 23:34, 43.

with a vision largely unrealized and holy expectations unfulfilled, even though he had accomplished all he could.[4] At the very end the next step is God's to take. No matter the unfinished character of our lives or how unredeemed our world still feels, we still have to pray and to age like prophets, never abandoning our heart's protest over the injustice and structural evil human beings have been forced to submit to. An illuminating model here might be Paul in chains, an apostle physically constricted but inwardly embracing the world to which he felt himself crucified.[5] The mystic side of the prophetic/mystic axis becomes more pronounced, but the mystic's passion draws its religious energy from the prophetic pole of our experience.

The more we think about the world—from the HIV-scourged populations of Africa to families languishing in the refugee camps of Ethiopia and Jenin, from the remembrance of killing fields in Cambodia to the memory of the disappeared of Argentina's "dirty war"—the more the human scene is going to appear to us as a "fierce landscape."[6] And whatever "solace" comes from "fierce landscapes"—at least so far as prophets are concerned—can only be the grace of discovering the risen Jesus within them. Paul wrote, "For the love of Christ urges us on" (2 Cor 5:14). The RSV and REB translate the Greek verb in this text [*synechei*] as "controls," the NAB as "impels," the NIV as "compels," and the JB as "overwhelms."[7] But what exactly does the love of Christ push, compel, impel, or urge us to? The answer may come in the next verse where Paul says (following the NRSV) "so that those who live might live no longer for themselves, but for him who died and was raised for them." The love of Christ—the love we have for him as well as the love he has for us—so "overwhelms" or "controls" us that we live for him, even as he died (and lived) for us. But how exactly do we live for Christ? We live for Christ insofar as we live for others, which is what Jesus did. And how can we live for others without stepping into those "fierce landscapes" where the others are to be found? In other words, does the love we have for Jesus impel or drive us into that world where death, whether by literal or metaphorical crucifixion, is an

---

4. John 19:30.

5. Gal 5:14.

6. See Belden C. Lane, *The Solace of Fierce Landscapes: Exploring Desert and Mountain Spirituality* (New York: Oxford University Press, 1998). I believe that geography and physical surroundings do indeed shape and shade a person's spirituality, but while oceans, mountains, deserts, and forests are places where one may find God I would not recommend them as places to find the risen Jesus.

7. The Good News Bible reads: "We are ruled by the love of Christ."

ever-present possibility? In short, as we grow older in the Spirit, we become not less prophetic but more so; not less like the Jesus constantly "on the way" in order to be among his people but more.

Spiritual directors understand why it is absolutely impossible to reach the "pre-Easter" Jesus, no matter how strenuously a person meditates and prays or no matter how excited the imagination becomes as it recreates gospel scenes. Five lifetimes in the land of Israel would bring the pre-Easter Jesus no closer than pictures in a scrapbook. The only Jesus available to the Church is Jesus risen—the Jesus who resides through the Spirit in the hearts of believers, in the assembly that gathers in his name, in the sacraments that bear his sign, and in the men and women who endure the marks of crucifixion. In this sense, the early Church moved beyond the pre-Easter Jesus, but the evangelists uniformly insist on the continuity of mission, message, and spiritual form between the one who was raised and the one who was baptized at the Jordan.

The language about a preferential option for the poor dismays many earnest Christians because they know they are not poor in any material sense, yet they do not believe they should be any less acceptable to God on that account. In response I try to explain that parents who have a child sick in the hospital by no means love their healthy children any less, but the sick daughter or son has a greater need of the parents' presence. Parents naturally become super-conscious of the child in distress. That the divine eye should be especially sensitive to human beings who are suffering is hardly surprising in itself, but that certain forms of suffering catch God's attention so quickly is theologically very significant and bound to affect the way we relate to God in prayer.

Curiously enough, given how intently the book of Job grapples with the mystery of undeserved suffering, "God" in the book—not as holy mystery but as a literary character—does not seem particularly bothered by the wretchedness that has befallen poor Job. On the other hand, the spiritual premise of many of the psalms is that God is deeply concerned about the sickness and other personal calamities that strike us. Otherwise, why pray to this God? The God of Exodus as well as the God of the prophets becomes so engaged, even angered, by the oppression the people of Israel suffer that the divine eye seems to notice little else. Now, where does this leave those of us who are not among the ranks of the victims of oppression? How much of a claim can we make upon divine attention? It leaves us with the choice of whether to stay at home or to join our parents at the hospital bedside, with a choice between solidarity and withdrawal. In this sense, as Gustavo Gutiérrez reminds us, the option for the poor is not at all "optional"—neither for ordinary Christians nor for spiritual directors.

Solidarity Presupposes Repentance

Before this dynamic connection between looking for God and discovering the crucified ones strikes the reader as special pleading, unfaithful to the diversity or rich texture of Christian experience, guilt-producing, or excessively kataphatic, I should point out that no one should set out on the path of discipleship who is not prepared to act upon the second part of Jesus' proclamation "repent, and believe in the good news" (Mark 1:15). In response to their having been called the first time the disciples embarked on a journey with Jesus in the course of which their performance was less than admirable or exemplary. By the end of the story one had betrayed Jesus, another had denied him, and all had fled. What Jesus said of Peter would certainly have been applicable to all of them: "For you are setting your mind not on divine things but on human things" (Mark 8:33). They would later argue about which of them was the greatest[8] and who most deserved the two seats of honor.[9] After their collapse, of course, the risen Jesus regroups them and calls them for the second time "to be with him, and to be sent out to proclaim the message" (Mark 3:14)—the same Jesus who has joined the one reading or listening to the Markan narrative and whose voice is to be heard in every passage.

Just like the disciples themselves, everyone of us needs to hear that "second call."[10] At the very least we need to be forewarned that our response to the first call might not be sufficient to keep us from later "setting our minds on human things." Why? Because the way of discipleship is going to entail a confrontation with one's own sinfulness and resistance.

---

8. Mark 9:33-37.

9. Mark 10:35-45.

10. "Second call" is not exactly the same as the "second journey" motif. See Gerald O'Collins, *The Second Journey: Spiritual Awareness and the Mid-Life Crisis* (Dublin: Villa Books, 1979). "Second call" belongs to the paschal experience and is thus intimately connected with forgiveness. On this point see Rowan Williams, *Resurrection: Interpreting the Easter Gospel* (Harrisburg, Penn.: Morehouse Publishing, 1994).

There is something Jesus must do for us that we cannot do for ourselves. Such is the unanimous testimony of the New Testament because such had been the experience of the earliest Christian communities. No one, consequently, would object to the claim that looking for God will inevitably entail a sustained engagement with personal sinfulness. The gospel pattern and the record of Christian experience are just too plain.

On what grounds, therefore, could anyone object to there being a connection between looking for God—following Jesus—and coming face to face with the poor? Here I am drawing on the schematizing of Christian experience that we find in the Spiritual Exercises. The one making the Exercises, despite great good will, cannot plunge right into the Third Week as a companion with Jesus in his suffering. For the reason why Jesus is on the cross—and the reason why there are victims in the first place—has something to do with the disorder that exists in one's own life, thoughts, and desires. The love that is so mysteriously revealed from the cross abbreviates for us both what the practice of solidarity means and what it could cost, but like everything else in Christian life, solidarity builds upon conversion. I would wager, however, that the conversion leading to solidarity will not occur and cannot be maintained without personal contact with the "other" who comes to us from the world of the poor. The gospel images of cloth shrinking, threads pulling, wine fermenting, and wineskins stretching—metaphors for the spiritual tugging and sweating that are part of learning to understand things afresh—remain ever so appropriate.[11] In the case of the Twelve, the wine had spilled and the rips in their cloaks had worsened as they attempted to live out their "first call."

Finding God in a Time of Disruption

I have already called attention to the sense of disruption that winds through Mark's Gospel. This might not sound like a particularly noteworthy trait of the narrative until we reflect on how persistently disruptive events appear there. But disruptions should be distinguished from interruptions.

---

11. I realize that the point of Jesus' comparison had to do with saving the old cloak, not making its tear worse, and preserving the old wineskins, not allowing them to be ruined and the wine lost (see Matt 9:17). Still, Jesus was responding to the perceived contrast in terms of a model of holiness between the religious professionals (John the Baptist and his followers, the Pharisees and their followers) and himself. His example was problematic to say the least, and if he was right about the proximity of the reign then his example and the teaching that explained it would also have been disruptive.

Interruptions are a familiar part of daily life and not infrequently turn out to be moments of grace, even when the interruptions are unwelcome or unpleasant. Disruptions, however, are marked by serious spiritual, mental, or emotional dislocation. Perhaps we should call them interruptions with an attitude. Interruptions tend to be momentary or occasional; afterwards routine takes over once again. Disruptions are attended by effects that linger and reconfigure the future. Paul's encounter with the risen Jesus was from all accounts sharply disruptive of what he would later call his "previous life,"[12] though not so disruptive that he would abandon his Jewishness. And how could he? The Jesus he discovered and loved was a Jew. In terms of large-scale events, the sixth-century B.C.E. exile in Babylon certainly constituted a horrendous disruption, the second-century efforts of the Seleucids under Antiochus Epiphanes IV to eradicate Jewish traditions constituted another, and the siege and destruction of Jerusalem by the Roman army in 66–70 represent yet a third.

The calling of the disciples represents more than a momentary disturbance in their routine near and around the Lake, the voice of John the Baptist was surely disruptive for Herod's government-as-usual. Howling loudly and fearsomely, the demons perceived in Jesus' message a fiercely disruptive threat to their interests. The religious leadership quickly discovered a disruption in the received way of thinking about Sabbath observance and the mediation of divine forgiveness. And "the desolating sacrilege set up where it ought not to be" (Mark 13:14) would be so disruptive that flight from Jerusalem would be the only way to survive.

The death of Jesus reflects a major disruptive moment in Mark's Gospel. In the cross one is confronted with the humiliation and execution of the Son of God, yet who in their right mind could have imagined *that* end to the story of God's arrival in the human world? But the premier disruption was the discovery of an empty tomb. The tomb's being empty revealed that things had never been the way they seemed while one first listened to the story of Jesus. Death is to be expected; death by crucifixion, horrifying as it is, is nonetheless historically comprehensible. The empty tomb, however, turned out to be not a pathway into eternity but the sign that Jesus was abiding among the living. The normal connection between life and death had been severed and the validity of everyday perceptions had been undermined.

12. Gal 1:13.

From this reading of Mark I would conclude that it is important to pay close attention to the fissures in our experience—those segments in our personal histories which make no sense or appear totally unconnected to the rest of our lives—if we want to find God. Yet God is not the disruption. God does not cause historical trauma. God is not "in" historical events any more than God is "in" a work of art or musical performance. As Elijah learned, God was not to be found in rock-splitting wind or in the shaking of the earth or in the fire, but in "a sound of sheer silence" (1 Kings 19:12). Nevertheless, fissures, collisions, and disruptions often serve to intensify the search for God enormously and prime us to hear the silence that follows.

In their commentary on the Gospel of Mark, John Donahue and Daniel Harrington draw attention to the words "The days will come when the bridegroom is taken away from them" (Mark 3:20) and the text's obvious allusion to Isaiah: "By a perversion of justice he was taken away" (53:8). They comment:

> The tension, and often incompatibility, between the old and the new is part of every religious tradition and attends every change within that tradition. Matthew and Luke wrestled with it and adapted it to their community situation. Contemporary Christians have no less a challenge.[13]

But, we may ask, does not the forcible removal of the bridegroom imply something more serious than incompatibility and tension? To be sure, the action of stretching and tearing apart could aptly describe the situation of faith in a time of cultural upheaval. But what we appear to be witnessing is nothing less than a gradual rending of the grand religious narrative that for centuries served to locate us in an unimaginably large and cold universe. The forced removal of the bridegroom—evoking the figure of God as Israel's "husband"—anticipates the arrest and execution of Jesus, and with the "disappearance" of Jesus, the community will enter its permanent fasting season. And so we face the erosion of a sustaining faith narrative on the one hand and the summary removal of Jesus on the other: in either case a disciple starts to feel light- headed and disoriented, like a person who has not eaten for some time.

---

13. John R. Donahue and Daniel J. Harrington, *The Gospel of Mark*, Sacra Pagina Series, 2 (Collegeville, Minn.: The Liturgical Press, 2002) 109.

Constructing a Fresh Version of the Narrative of Faith

If the deconstructionists and postmodernists are correct, the sense that reality is breaking into fragments of meaning and that no culture, no religion, and no ideology can ever again lay claim to being normative is bound to get more severe. In such a context, the ministry of spiritual direction—in the various forms it can take—stands to play a highly significant role. In fact, the current interest in this ministry goes beyond the need felt by many to retrieve the experiential dimension of Christian faith. The interest reflects, I believe, the various dislocations that have been touching all of us in one way or another but which have been felt in acute ways by women and men for whom finding God has become life's most pressing concern. The process of spiritual direction not only furnishes people the opportunity to discern the presence of God in their lives but also to see the pattern of grace that has been unfolding over many years. Frequently in the process of direction people "write" their stories.

Every human life is a unique story; with nuance and distinctiveness, each of those narratives recapitulates the history of salvation. Whether we are conscious of doing so or not, we spend a lifetime composing a generally unwritten account of who and what we are. We make plans, choose careers, enter relationships, change direction, raise and support families. In the process we experience countless interruptions and a significant number of disruptions. Either of these could derail us, although sometimes troubling and unsettling moments actually help us stay on track, under the principle that "all things work together for good for those who love God" (Rom 8:28).

The bottom line, however, is that we both crave and create order, and spontaneously resist whatever interrupts or disrupts. To reflect on one's life, therefore, is to look for pattern and connections, to notice the stitching that secures the various patches and seams—the events, circumstances and situations, relationships and feelings, failures, suffering and consolations—that together constitute the history of our salvation. And those patterns and connections reach beyond the personal to the global drama in which the mystery of divine revelation displays itself. For people of faith God is the ultimate source of order and reasonableness. "God" explains us. The narratives of creation in Genesis, deliverance in Exodus, and divine engagement in the prophetic literature and historical books allow us to visualize our place in the world and furnish the categories by which we interpret our individual lives and human history. Relationships anchor us, too: our relationships with fellow seekers and travelers, with the community of faith, with the past by means of a tradition of belief, spirituality, and moral practice, with the deceased, and even with the future through the hope that binds and will forever bind together men and women who look for God. In spiritual direction, as I have said, one pays attention to how so many disparate moments are threaded together, while Scripture gives us both a lens through which to contemplate our lives and a vocabulary by which we can verbalize what we have noticed.

The stretching and rending of this fabric of faith, however, has taken its toll on all of us. The familiar pattern unravels. Or to vary the simile, the faith-world, perhaps a bit more easily than the social or cultural worlds we inhabit, can come unglued. This ungluing results from a variety of assaults against our confidence in the way things are supposed to fit together. Some people, not understanding the nature of the Gospels as religious texts, have been disillusioned by historical and literary studies. Others have suffered an erosion of confidence in church leadership for reasons all too obvious to those who read the newspaper. They are wary because they cannot always know right away which prophets—or pastors—come clothed like sheep "but inwardly are ravenous wolves" (Matt 7:15). The result is a weakening of ecclesial identity, perhaps even a reluctance to be identified as Catholic. Still others have reached the conclusion that no one religion can be the way to God and from that relativistic position have deconstructed for themselves the church's central claims about Jesus. And so on. But the assaults arise from other corners as well—the debilitating individualism of North Atlantic culture, the long-term corrosive effect of finding fulfillment in being consumers, or our creeping reluctance to meet other human beings beyond the safety of social, ethnic, and cultural boundaries. People sense something is wrong with their lives but may not know how to diagnose the problem, except to say that the gospel seems increasingly out of touch, irrelevant. Which is, of course, to confound the symptoms with the remedy.

The glue, on the other hand, consists of longing and desire. The Spirit's pull is experienced as desire, but desire is seeded in us and eventually crystallizes only when the story of faith is preached. In a letter written in 1536 to a Benedictine nun, Ignatius gave this advice:

> After recounting your weaknesses and fears, which are very much to the point, you say, "I am a poor religious; I *think* I desire to serve Christ our

Lord." You lack the courage to say, "I desire to serve Christ our Lord," or, "The Lord gives me desires to serve him." Instead you say, "I *think* I desire to serve him." If you reflect, you will realize that these desires to serve Christ our Lord do not come from yourself but are given by the Lord. And so when you say, "The Lord gives me strong desires to serve him," it is the Lord himself you are praising by making known his gift; it is he and not yourself in whom you boast, since you do not attribute the grace to yourself. [14]

So far as Ignatius was concerned, the vitality of one's interior life is to be gauged by the quality and depth of our desires *to serve*. Or to state the point more sharply and concretely, by the depth and quality of our desire to be where Jesus is, since "where I am, there will my servant be also" (John 12:26). And here it is important to note two things. First, not every inclination toward a specific form of service can be realized. Not only do desires have to be prioritized, but there is no guarantee that every holy desire, even if it comes from God, is supposed to be fulfilled. In many cases desires orient us toward choices and actions, yet perhaps just as frequently our desires are simply revealing the richness and complexity of our interior lives. Second, joining oneself interiorly to all the crucified ones is a privileged way of being with Jesus and thus of realizing a holy desire. If, therefore, the religious desire that pervades our lives is the desire for union with God, then it is essential to remember that the desire for God always has as its corollary a desire for union with God's people. A fresh version of the narrative of faith would have as its premise that one's relationship with God grows in the measure that one lives the preferential option for the poor.

To return then to our theme, the disruption which has come to mark the lives of so many people today may be showing itself in terms of the difference between what we seek at the deepest level of our heart's longing and the mounting crises—political, economic, cultural, and social—in which the world finds itself. And these crises have only been compounded by the current ecclesiastical problems which threaten to split the narrative of faith from the Church that was commissioned to preach it. All of us want to experience the love of God—the love that brought "me" into existence yet which is at the same time the love that brings "us" into being, too. And love, we have reason to hope, can mediate the sense of disruption, fragmentation, and disorder. Spiritual direction certainly cannot

14. See *Ignatius of Loyola: Spiritual Exercises and Selected Works*, ed. George E. Ganss (Mahwah, N.J.: Paulist Press, 1991) 334. Emphasis added.

afford to overlook the experience of existence itself coming unstuck or dissolving into fragments, and it would be unrealistic to think that we can make this cultural experience go away simply by putting our trust in God. What direction can do, however, is assist those for whom the experience of disruption has been all too real to "write" the narrative of their lives. That the resulting story may have certain structural analogies with the Gospel of Mark ought not to be surprising. Its notes of urgency, disruption, conflict and confrontation, resistance, misperception, and apocalyptic—together with its unyielding insistence that Jesus is not among the dead—can help us to name what has been happening to us.

For some people the rhetoric about finding or rejecting God boils down to the need to discern the proper moral response to an experience of God's love. Maybe they just find it easier to do than to pray, or maybe they harbor the prejudice that prayer is not practical unless it leads to action. We should anticipate, naturally enough, that religious experience is going to have a moral or practical derivative: action is "right" insofar as it is consistent with the divine love we have experienced. But to push the insight a little further, our experience of God also draws us toward people (not that much urging is needed)—praying for them, remembering them, working alongside them, ministering to them, keeping the poor at the center of our concern and never allowing them to drift off the radar of awareness. Needless to say, every Christian cannot be in the same spiritual place at the same time. Religious experience is a process, not just a series of discrete moments; inner events flow back and forth into each other. Overall, however, the flow moves in a specific direction insofar as the gospel becomes the channel through which experience flows. Conversion is the universal starting point and effective oneness with others in the risen Jesus remains the goal.

Human salvation is not a matter of countless millions of men and women playing individual games or giving solo performances. If that were the case, then the Church would be nothing more than a giant sports arena or a classroom; it could never be a sacrament or sign of the close union between God and the human race.[15] Salvation, rather, is a corporate project, a joint mission in which the stakes of each individual are the stakes of all. Those who are engaged in the ministry of spiritual direction

15. The Dogmatic Constitution on the Church (*Lumen Gentium*) No. 1.

have the singular grace of accompanying others as they compose the narrative of their lives. They watch and listen as women and men discover the mystery of God through the continuities and perhaps ever more so through the discontinuities of their lives. If the Gospel of Mark has any particular relevance for the ministry of spiritual direction today, perhaps it is that one does not need a fully self-consistent narrative in order to get one's life together, a comprehensive viewpoint that ties together all loose ends and makes sense of the dead-ends one has encountered along the way. Even a faith that shows itself in fragments can make us whole. For the fragments coalesce around desire and that desire for wholeness and communion is awakened and fed by the Spirit of Jesus risen.

Should Christian spirituality move beyond Jesus? If someone is wondering whether Christians might be able to gain new insight into humanity's interior life from men and women who belong to other religious traditions, I believe the answer should be yes. If one is wondering whether there is more to the divine mystery than what is to be experienced by encountering the God of Israel in the Jesus of the Gospels, I would answer that religious experience displays itself many different forms; there are obviously a large number of distinct ways of relating to the divine mystery. People can certainly experience God apart from Jesus. If the question is asking whether religious experiences ultimately converge in a mystical oneness, I would answer what appears attractive speculatively overlooks the determinative nature of the particular and concrete.

This is not the place to undertake a comparative theology of the world religions or to look at the formally christological issues about salvation, although I believe that spiritual directors—women and men who work in the Spirit's laboratory—may have valuable insights to contribute to that ongoing scholarly conversation.[16] What applies the brakes to a theoretical convergence of religions at the level of mystical union with the divine, it

16. The key question has generally been whether and in what way we can claim that Jesus is the universal savior in a religiously pluralistic world. See, for instance, Jacques Dupuis, *Christianity and the Religions: From Confrontation to Dialogue* (Maryknoll, N.Y.: Orbis Books, 2002) 163–94. I can only suggest that maybe there is no way of reaching a satisfactory answer to this question if we start with the universal claim (Jesus is the one mediator or unique savior) and then move to the concrete (how does this saving action show itself in the lives of those who are not Christian). If we reverse the process by starting with the concrete, historical, everyday experience of salvation as Christians know it, then the theological issue is not going to be one of uniqueness and squaring our dogmatic claims with what has been happening in the other world religions. The theological issue becomes instead the distinctiveness of the Christian religion experience.

seems to me, is the prophetic pole of the Christian experience and the insertion of our imagination in the historical fortune of God's people. There are multiple ways of finding God; finding God in Jesus is one of those ways. But as we have noted already, the first disciples once knew God apart from Jesus, too. The point we have to keep attending to, therefore, is the difference Jesus makes—and the differences that make Jesus.

Postscript
A Certain Tension

A well-known and intriguing passage in Exodus 34 recounts how Moses would receive words from God which he would then deliver to the Israelites, but Moses' face had become so radiant from being in the LORD's presence that he had to cover it:

> When Moses had finished speaking with them, he put a veil over his face; but whenever Moses went in before the LORD to speak with him, he would take the veil off, until he came out, and when he came out, and told the Israelites what had been commanded, the Israelites would see the face of Moses, that the skin of his face was shining; and Moses would put the veil on his face again, until he went in to speak with him (Exod 34:33-35).

On the basis of such special effects, who would ever dare to question Moses either at that time or any other time in the religious history of Israel? Whatever Moses said was law, for it came directly from God. Moses—and presumably his successors, since the "scribes and the Pharisees sit on Moses' seat" (Matt 23:2)—held supreme authority when it came to articulating the will of God. All the more striking, therefore, is the equally well-known passage in the second letter to the Corinthians where Paul allegorizes the Exodus text:

> Since, then, we have such a hope, we act with great boldness, not like Moses, who put a veil over his face to keep the people of Israel from gazing at the end of the glory that was being set aside. But their minds were hardened. Indeed, to this very day, when they hear the reading of the old covenant, that same veil is still there, since only in Christ is it set aside. Indeed, to this very day whenever Moses is read, a veil lies over their minds; but when one turns to the Lord the veil is removed. Now the Lord is the Spirit,

and where the Spirit of the Lord is, there is freedom. And all of us, with
unveiled faces, seeing the glory of the Lord as though reflected in a mirror,
are being transformed into the same image from one degree of glory to another; for this comes from the Lord, the Spirit (2 Cor 3:12-18).

It seems to me that Paul, whose authority as an apostle did not derive
from "Moses' seat" but came directly from the God who called him, is
making a quintessentially New Testament claim about religious experience. Between the believer and the divine mystery there stands no intermediary. The image of "unveiled faces" suggests that those who are living
"in Christ" are in fact standing in the divine presence. Christ himself is
the perfect reflection of the mystery of God, and thus those who daily
keep the eyes of their heart fixed on Christ become transformed into the
image they have been contemplating. The displacement of Moses in this
way as authoritative voice was a major theological step. Not only did this
step remove Moses as the major conduit of revelation; it also affirmed the
integrity of the individual's experience of God. The New Testament is
quite clear, of course, that the Church has a structure, for the good of
order, and that intercessory prayer on behalf of others remains an important expression of faith and solidarity. Nevertheless, through the Spirit
women and men come to know God for themselves.

The Exodus text could be counterpointed, however, with an equally
well-known passage from Deuteronomy:

> Surely, this commandment that I am commanding you today is not too
> hard for you, nor is it too far away. It is not in heaven, that you should say,
> "Who will go up to heaven for us, and get it for us so that we may hear it
> and observe it?" Neither is it beyond the sea, that you should say, "Who
> will cross to the other side of the sea for us, and get it for us so that we may
> hear it and observe it?" No, the word is very near to you; it is in your
> mouth and in your heart for you to observe (Deut 30:11-14).

What further need is there for intermediaries, for select individuals to be
bearers of special messages from God? It could be argued, I suppose, that
the text is simply referring to the way the divine law gets imprinted on the
minds and hearts of those who choose life. Yet the fact that "the word is very
near" invites us to think that there is more involved here than the acquiring
of spiritual software. The word is in our hearts not because God placed it
there but because God speaks it there. This fact, as I explained at the outset,
is truly the presupposition of spiritual direction—the condition for its pos-

sibility and the reason why men and women seek out other Christians who can help them "hear" what the divine "voice" is saying. The divine "saying" necessarily occurs in a context, not in an historical or cultural vacuum. There is no laboratory-pure interior space—a space fully cleansed of the human particularities that distinguish each of us—where the divine voice can be listened to in a religiously antiseptic, unimpeded fashion.

While the spiritual director is by no means an intermediary, neither is the director merely a sounding board. Faith speaks *to* faith and faith speaks *from* faith, for the one listening seeks the face of God as earnestly as the one who is sharing and confiding. There are numerous consolations along the way, that is, experiences which confirm that we have really encountered the mystery of God or that we have surely taken the way that leads to life. Among those experiences I believe that the sense of being in communion and solidarity with other human beings, especially with the poor and most especially with victims, belongs very close to the top of the list. To experience oneself as moved with compassion is an important grace, and experiencing oneself as incomprehensibly loved by God is still another. For compassion enables us to forgive, to accompany, to share, and to serve, while knowing God's love humbles the mind, lifts burdens, sets spirits free, and engenders generosity.

What we do not know, however, is what is ultimately going to happen to our world. The contours of our union with the divine mystery in the next life is something we can only speculate about. What we can insist on, however, is that the present life is not a mere transition to the next, as if creation, human history, the particular fortunes of people and their societies should not be taken all that seriously because we are simply hitch-hiking through time. When it comes to thinking about the future, Scripture engages in exercises of "hopeful imagination," although the end is often imagined to be preceded by events of apocalyptic proportions. Here and now, though, we should be doing all we can to avoid the calamities of war and pestilence, to rid the world of the political and social decay on which despair and terrorism feed, to confront evil and injustice head-on precisely so that we do not wind up destroying ourselves and rendering the planet unfit for human habitation. In short, we do not begin reflecting on the nature of God by speculating about the glory that awaits us after death. We must start with the aspirations we have for this world and discern the Spirit's redemptive action among us now.

The risen Jesus, we firmly believe, still accompanies his disciples, not in order to show them how to walk through life with their souls unscratched but to empower them to keep their feet firmly planted in the earth. I think of grandparents. As they get older and have to reckon with the prospect of leaving the world, their desire that the world should be a secure place where their grandchildren—and all grandchildren—can walk the streets without fear of being stalked, or stepping on landmines, or seduced by drugs—that desire grows only stronger, holier, and more fervent. Such desire is a telling sign, we know, of generativity and the triumph of the human spirit. None of us can claim any special insight into what comes next, after this life; we can only talk about what we have garnered from the content and pressure of our deepest yearnings. And if we have ever truly loved other human beings, then there is no way of separating the part of our imagination that configures what we hope for from the people who matter to us and whom we shall have to leave behind. How remarkably, reassuringly human, then, that Jesus risen has promised to remain among his sisters and brothers "to the end of the age" (Matt 28:20).

Once we acknowledge that the Spirit of God alone—the Spirit which for us bears a Jesus imprint—penetrates human lives and speaks within the recesses of a person's mind, heart and memory, then we have no choice but to allow that Spirit to lead, direct, and shape the life of everyone who is seeking God. Or to frame the point on a scale a little less grand, we have no choice but to respect the freedom of others to respond to the Spirit in whatever ways they discern to be best. Thus the way our faith lives commence in our initial youthful sensitivity to the presence of God and what we eventually grow into might be awfully far apart, and nothing guarantees that the discernments of a lifetime will always be flawless. Deception is bound to arise, and it is usually subtle; light and darkness sometimes feel indistinguishable. Yet the Spirit does not simply move; it moves in a "direction," which is why I said it bears a Jesus imprint. Many things are written in Scripture, not all of which are about Jesus. This may explain why Luke writes: "Then beginning with Moses and all the prophets, he interpreted to them *all the things about himself in all the scriptures*" (Luke 24:27). So too in a human life. Many things are "written" there, but not all of them are about Jesus. We certainly need to be a praying people, therefore, and we may often have recourse to spiritual direction in order to interpret those events and circumstances of our lives that are about Jesus.

For their part, directors can expect to live within a certain tension, namely, the tension between their Christian belief that the Spirit is irreversibly the Spirit of Jesus and their religious conviction about the sovereignty of each individual's interior space. Without realizing it, Paul might even have stumbled upon and thereby drawn attention to this tension in his words "where the Spirit of the Lord is, there is freedom." I don't think he anticipated that this very Spirit could leave a person free to pursue quite a different religious path. Yet grace is seeded into the human world in marvelously diverse ways.

If it should happen therefore that a person finds herself drawn outside the Christian circle—a prospect we need to be prepared for the more the world religions engage each other,—then a wise director is not going to intrude on the way the mystery of God is unfolding in the other person's life. A text that might come to mind is the story of the exorcist who expels demons in Jesus' name yet does not walk in the company of Jesus' followers—but Mark 9:38 would not apply in the case of someone who is moving further from living and acting in Jesus' name. The dynamic under way in another's interior life could prove both challenging for the director and distressing; watching a person whom we have been accompanying step onto a different religious path is bound to make us revisit our own loyalties and convictions. The words "No one can come to me unless drawn by the Father who sent me" (John 6:44) furnish little comfort. Still, I would urge that in the process of directing or accompanying others the focus question "Where is God in your life?" remains incomplete without "Where are God's people?" The question "What is God like for you?" needs as a follow-up "Who exactly are the people you allow to step into your soul?" The Spirit of Jesus orients us toward the people of God—which may account for why someone who has learned Jesus' name would want to drive out demons from societies, neighborhoods, and individual lives. The determinacy of the director's own religious identity, so suffused with Scripture, gospel and liturgy, ought to enhance his or her sensitivity to the presence of mystery in our world. At the same time, this very determinacy sharpens the director's awareness of every death by crucifixion and the particular places where God has chosen to join the human story. And here, perhaps, is where the Christian's song of adoration takes its pitch.

Bibliography

Aquinas, Thomas. *Summa Theologiae*. Torino, Italy: Edizioni Paoline, 1988.

Argentina. Comisión Nacional sobre la Desaparición de Personas. *Nunca más: The Report of the Argentine National Commission on the Disappeared*. New York: Farrar, Straus and Giroux, 1986.

Armstrong, Karen. *Buddha*. New York: Penguin Putnam Inc., 2001.

———. *Islam: A Short History*. New York: Random House, 2000.

Ashley, James Matthew. *Interruptions: Mysticism, Politics, and Theology in the Work of Johann Baptist Metz*. Notre Dame: University of Notre Dame Press, 1998.

Augustine. *The Confessions*. Trans. Henry Chadwick. New York: Oxford University Press, 1991.

———. *Tractates on the First Epistle of John*. Trans. John W. Retting. The Fathers of the Church Series, vol. 92. Washington, D.C.: Catholic University of America Press, 1995.

Barnes, Michael. "The Guru in Hinduism." *The Way* 24:2 (1984) 146–53.

Barry, William A. *Spiritual Direction and the Encounter with God: A Theological Inquiry*. Mahwah, N.J.: Paulist Press, 1992.

Barry, William A., and William J. Connolly. *The Practice of Spiritual Direction*. New York: Seabury Press, 1982.

Beresford, David. *Ten Men Dead: The Story of the 1981 Irish Hunger Strike*. New York: Atlantic Monthly Press, 1997.

Bochen, Christine M., ed. *Thomas Merton: Essential Writings*. Maryknoll, N.Y.: Orbis Books, 2000.

Borg, Marcus. *Conflict, Holiness and Politics in the Teachings of Jesus*. Harrisburg, Penn.: Trinity Press International, 1998.

Brown, Raymond E. *The Gospel According to John I–XII*. The Anchor Bible. New York: Doubleday & Co., 1966.

Byrne, Lavinia. "When to Stop." *The Way*, Supplement 54 (Autumn 1985) 51–59.

Caputo, John D. "Apostles of the Impossible: On God and the Gift in Derrida and Marion." In *God, the Gift, and Postmodernism.* Ed. John D. Caputo and Michael J. Scanlon, 185–222. Bloomington, Ind.: Indiana University Press, 1999.

Chadwick, Graham. "Giving the Exercises and Training Directors in an Ecumenical Context." *The Way* Supplement 68 (Summer 1990) 35–41.

Clancy, Thomas. *The Conversational Word of God: A Commentary on the Doctrine of St. Ignatius of Loyola concerning Spiritual Conversation, with Four Early Jesuit Texts.* St. Louis: The Institute of Jesuit Sources, 1978.

Clooney, Francis X. "A Charism for Dialogue: Advice from the Early Jesuit Missionaries in Our World of Religious Pluralism." *Studies in the Spirituality of Jesuits* 34:2 (2002).

———. "In Ten Thousand Places, in Every Blade of Grass: Uneventful but True Confessions about Finding God in India, and Here Too." *Studies in the Spirituality of Jesuits* 28:3 (1996).

Connolly, William J. "Contemporary Spiritual Direction: Scope and Principles." *Studies in the Spirituality of Jesuits* 7:3 (1978).

Connolly, William J., and Madeline Birmingham. *Witnessing to the Fire: Spiritual Direction and the Development of Directors, One Center's Experience.* Kansas City, Mo.: Sheed & Ward, 1994.

Connolly, William J., and Philip Land. "Jesuit Spiritualities and the Struggle for Social Justice." *Studies in the Spirituality of Jesuits* 9:4 (1977).

Cornille, Catherine. *The Guru in Indian Catholicism: Ambiguity or Opportunity of Inculturation?* Grand Rapids, Mich.: Wm. B. Eerdmans, 1991. Louvain: Peeters Press, 1991.

———, ed. *Many Mansions?: Multiple Religious Belonging and Christian Identity.* Maryknoll, N.Y.: Orbis Books, 2002.

Cousins, Ewert. "The Nature of Faith in Interreligious Dialogue." *The Way* Supplement 78 (1993) 32–41.

Culligan, Kevin. *Spiritual Direction: Contemporary Readings.* Locust Valley, N.Y.: Living Flame Press, 1983.

Cunningham, Lawrence S., and Keith J. Egan. *Christian Spirituality: Themes from the Tradition.* Mahwah, N.J.: Paulist Press, 1996.

Damasio, Antonio. *Looking for Spinoza: Joy, Sorrow, and the Feeling Brain.* Orlando, Fla.: Harcourt, Inc., 2003.

Das, A. Andrew, and Frank J. Matera. *The Forgotten God: Perspectives in Biblical Theology.* Louisville, Ky.: Westminster John Knox Press, 2002.

Dawe, Donald G., and John B. Carman, eds. *Christian Faith in a Religiously Plural World.* Maryknoll, N.Y.: Orbis Books, 1978.

D'Costa, Gavin. *The Meeting of Religions and the Trinity.* Maryknoll, N.Y.: Orbis Books, 2000.

————, ed. *Christian Uniqueness Reconsidered: The Myth of a Pluralistic Theology of Religions*. Maryknoll, N.Y.: Orbis Books, 1990.

Dehne, Carl. "Popular Devotions." *The New Dictionary of Sacramental Worship*. Ed. Peter Fink, 331–40. Collegeville, Minn.: The Liturgical Press, 1990.

Donahue, John R., and Daniel J. Harrington. *The Gospel of Mark*. Sacra Pagina Series, 2. Collegeville, Minn.: The Liturgical Press, 2002.

Donoghue, Denis. "God's Will: Where Desires Commingle." *Review for Religious* 60:6 (2001) 647–54.

Downey, Michael. *Understanding Christian Spirituality*. Mahwah, N.J.: Paulist Press, 1997.

Dulles, Avery. "Faith and Revelation." In *Systematic Theology: Roman Catholic Perspectives*, ed. Francis Schüssler Fiorenza and John P. Galvin, vol. 1:89-128. Minneapolis: Fortress Press, 1991.

Dunn, James D. G. *Jesus and the Spirit: A Study of the Religious and Charismatic Experience of Jesus and the First Christians as Reflected in the New Testament*. Philadelphia: The Westminster Press, 1975.

————. *The Partings of the Ways between Christianity and Judaism and Their Significance for the Character of Christianity*. Philadelphia: Trinity Press International, 1991.

Dunne, Tad. "Experience." In *Dictionary of Catholic Spirituality*. Ed. Michael Downey, 365–77. Collegeville, Minn.: The Liturgical Press, 1993.

Dupuis, Jacques. *Christianity and the Religions: From Confrontation to Dialogue*. Maryknoll, N.Y.: Orbis Books, 2002.

————. *Toward a Christian Theology of Religious Pluralism*. Maryknoll, N.Y.: Orbis Books, 1997.

Edwards, Tilden. *Spiritual Director, Spiritual Companion: Guide to Tending the Soul*. Mahwah, N.J.: Paulist Press, 2001.

————. *Spiritual Friend: Reclaiming the Gift of Spiritual Direction*. New York: Paulist Press, 1980.

Ehrman, Bart D. *Jesus: Apocalyptic Prophet of the New Millennium*. New York: Oxford University Press, 1999.

Evans, Linda Mary. "Catholic and Protestant Approaches to the First Week." *The Way* Supplement 68 (Summer 1990) 5–12.

Fagin, Gerald. "The Spirituality of the Spiritual Director." *Presence: Journal of Spiritual Directors International* 8:3 (2002) 7–14.

Fischer, Louis, ed. *The Essential Gandhi: An Anthology of His Writings in His Life, Work and Ideas*. New York: Vintage Books, 1983.

Fretheim, Terrence E. "Will of God in the OT." *The Anchor Bible Dictionary*. Ed. David Noel Freedman, 6:915-920. New York: Doubleday, 1992.

Galeano, Eduardo. *Open Veins of Latin America: Five Centuries of the Pillage of a Continent*. New York: Monthly Review Press, 1973.

Gallagher, Winifred. *Working on God.* New York: The Modern Library, 2000.

Gandhi, Mohandas K. *All Men Are Brothers: Life and Thoughts of Mahatma Gandhi as Told in His Own Words.* Ed. Krishna Kripalani. New York: Columbia University Press, 1969.

———. *Autobiography: The Story of My Experiments with Truth.* Trans. Mahadev Desai. New York: Dover Publications, Inc., 1983.

Goodier, Alban. *The Public Life of Our Lord Jesus Christ.* New York: P. J. Kenedy & Sons, 1931.

Gratton, Carolyn. "Spiritual Direction." *The New Dictionary of Catholic Spirituality.* Ed. Michael Downey, 911–16. Collegeville, Minn.: The Liturgical Press, 1993.

Gray, Donald. "The Real Absence: A Note on the Eucharist." In *Living Bread, Saving Cup: Readings on the Eucharist,* ed. Kevin Seasoltz, 190-196. Collegeville, Minn.: The Liturgical Press, 1982.

Greeley, Andrew. *The Catholic Imagination.* Berkeley, Calif.: University of California Press, 2000.

Grenz, Stanley J. *The Social God and the Relational Self: A Trinitarian Theology of the Imago Dei.* Louisville, Ky.: Westminster John Knox Press, 2001.

Griffiths, Paul J. *Christianity through Non-Christian Eyes.* Maryknoll, N.Y.: Orbis Books, 1990.

———. "The Uniqueness of Christian Doctrine Defended." In *Christian Uniqueness Reconsidered: The Myth of a Pluralistic Theology of Religions.* Ed. Gavin D'Costa, 157–73. Maryknoll, NY: Orbis Books, 1990.

Guibert, Joseph de. *The Theology of the Spiritual Life.* New York: Sheed and Ward, 1953.

Gutierrez, Gustavo. *The God of Life.* Maryknoll, N.Y.: Orbis Books, 1991.

———. *We Drink From Our Own Wells: The Spiritual Journey of a People.* Maryknoll, N.Y.: Orbis Books, 1984.

Haight, Roger. *Dynamics of Theology.* Maryknoll, N.Y.: Orbis Books, 2001; first published 1990.

Harrington, Daniel J. *The Gospel of Matthew.* Sacra Pagina Series, 1. Collegeville, Minn.: The Liturgical Press, 1991.

Hart, Kevin. "The Experience of God." In *The Religious.* Ed. John D. Caputo, 159–74. Malden, Mass.: Blackwell Publishers, Inc., 2002.

Hellwig, Monika. "Eschatology." In *Systematic Theology: Roman Catholic Perspectives.* Ed. Francis Schüssler Fiorenza and John P. Galvin, 2:349–72. Minneapolis: Fortress Press, 1991.

Hilkert, Mary Catherine. "*Imago Dei*: Does the Symbol Have a Future?" *The Santa Clara Lectures* 8:3 (April 14, 2002).

Hillesum, Etty. *An Interrupted Life and Letters from Westerbork*. New York: Henry Holt, 1996.

Horsley, Richard. *1 Corinthians*. Abingdon New Testament Commentaries. Nashville, Tenn.: Abingdon Press, 1998.

———. *Jesus and the Spiral of Violence: Popular Jewish Resistance in Roman Palestine*. Minneapolis: Fortress Press, 1993.

Huggett, Joyce. "Why Ignatian Spirituality Hooks Protestants." *The Way* Supplement 68 (Summer 1990) 22–34.

Iersel, Bas M. F. van. *Mark: A Reader-Response Commentary*. Trans. W. H. Bisscheroux. Journal for the Study of the New Testament Supplement Series 164. Sheffield: Sheffield Academic Press, 1998.

Ignatius, of Loyola, Saint. *Letters of St. Ignatius of Loyola*. Ed. William J. Young. Chicago: Loyola University Press, 1959.

———.*Ignatius of Loyola: The Spiritual Exercises and Selected Works*. Ed. George E. Ganss. Mahwah, N.J.: Paulist Press, 1991.

Ivens, Michael. "The Eighteenth Annotation and the Early Directories." *The Way* Supplement 48 (Spring 1983) 3–10.

Johnson, Luke Timothy. *Living Jesus: Learning the Heart of the Gospel*. New York: HarperCollins, 1999.

———. *The Real Jesus: The Misguided Quest for the Historical Jesus and the Truth of the Traditional Gospels*. New York: HarperCollins, 1996.

———. *Religious Experience in Earliest Christianity: A Missing Dimension in New Testament Studies*. Minneapolis: Fortress Press, 1998.

Jones, Alan. *Exploring Spiritual Direction*. Boston, Mass.: Cowley Publications, 1982; 1999.

Juergensmeyer, Mark. *Terror in the Mind of God: The Global Rise of Religious Violence*. Berkeley, Calif.: University of California Press, 2000.

Julian of Norwich. *Revelations of Divine Love*. Trans. Clifton Wolters. New York: Penguin Books, 1996.

Kilmartin, Edward. *The Eucharist in the West: History and Theology*. Ed. Robert J. Daly. Collegeville, Minn.: The Liturgical Press, 1998.

Kugel, James L. *The God of Old: Inside the Lost World of the Bible*. New York: The Free Press, 2003.

Lambrecht, Jan. *Second Corinthians*. Sacra Pagina Series, 8. Collegeville, Minn.: The Liturgical Press, 1999.

Lane, Belden C. *The Solace of Fierce Landscapes: Exploring Desert and Mountain Spirituality*. New York: Oxford University Press, 1998.

Lash, Nicholas. *Easter in Ordinary: Reflections on Human Experience and the Knowledge of God*. Charlottesville: University Press of Virginia, 1988.

LeBlanc, Adrian Nicole. *Random Family: Love, Drugs, Trouble, and Coming of Age in the Bronx.* New York: Scribner, 2003.

Leech, Kenneth. *Experiencing God: Theology as Spirituality.* New York: Harper & Row, 1985.

———. *The Eye of the Storm: Living Spirituality in the Real World.* New York: HarperCollins, 1992.

———. *Soul Friend: The Practice of Christian Spirituality.* New York: Harper & Row, 1977.

———. "Interrogating the Tradition." *The Way* Supplement 54 [*Approaches to Spiritual Direction* (Autumn 1985)] 10–20.

Lescher, Bruce. "Spiritual Direction: Stalking the Boundaries." In *Spirituality for Ministers*, vol. 2: *Perspectives for the 21ˢᵗ Century.* Ed. Robert J. Wicks, 315–26. Mahwah, N.J.: Paulist Press, 2000.

Lipner, Julius. "The 'Inter' of Interfaith Spirituality." *The Way* Supplement 78 (1993) 64–70.

Lohfink, Norbert. *Option for the Poor: The Basic Principles of Liberation Theology in the Light of the Bible.* 2ⁿᵈ ed. N. Richland Hills, Texas: BIBAL Press, 1995.

Lonergan, Bernard. *A Second Collection.* Philadelphia: The Westminster Press, 1974.

Lonsdale, David. "Spiritual Direction as Prophetic Ministry." In *Spirituality for Ministers*, vol. 2: *Perspectives for the 21ˢᵗ Century.* Ed. Robert J. Wicks, 327–42. Mahwah, N.J.: Paulist Press, 2000.

———. *Eyes to See, Ears to Hear: A Companion to the Spiritual Exercises of Saint Ignatius.* Chicago: Loyola Press, 1990, 1997.

Louf, André. *Grace Can Do More: Spiritual Accompaniment and Spiritual Growth.* Kalamazoo, Mich.: Cistercian Publications, 2002.

Louth, Andrew. *The Wilderness of God.* Nashville, Tenn.: Abingdon Press, 1991.

Malina, Bruce J., and Richard L. Rohrbaugh. *Social Science Commentary on the Synoptic Gospels.* Minneapolis: Fortress Press, 1992.

Martin, James, ed. *How Can I Find God?: The Famous and Not-So-Famous Consider the Quintessential Question.* Liguori, Mo.: Triumph Books, 1997.

Mays, James Luther. "The God Who Reigns." In *The Forgotten God: Perspectives in Biblical Theology.* Ed. A. Andrew Das and Frank J. Matera. Louisville, Ky.: Westminster John Knox Press, 2002.

McBrien, Richard P. *Catholicism: New Edition.* New York: HarperCollins, 1994.

McDonnell, Kilian. "Spirit and Experience in Bernard of Clairvaux." *Theological Studies* 58:1 (1997) 3–18.

McManus, Philip and Gerald Schlabach, eds. *Relentless Persistence: Nonviolent Action in Latin America.* Philadelphia: New Society Publishers, 1991.

Meier, John P. *A Marginal Jew: Rethinking the Historical Jesus.* Volume 1: *The Roots of the Problem and the Person.* New York: Doubleday, 1991.

Mellibovsky, Matilde. *Circle of Love Over Death: Testimonies of the Mothers of the Plaza de Mayo*. Willimantic, Conn.: Curbstone Press, 1997.

Merton, Thomas. *The Asian Journal of Thomas Merton*. Ed. Naomi Burton, Patrick Hart, and James Laughlin. New York: New Directions, 1973.

———. *Mystics and Zen Masters*. New York: Dell Publishing Co., 1967. 11th printing.

———. *New Seeds of Contemplation*. New York: New Directions Books, 1961.

———. *No Man Is an Island*. New York: Harcourt Brace Jovanovich, 1955. Reprint, New York: Barnes & Noble, 2003.

———. *Turning Towards the World: The Journals of Thomas Merton*. Ed. Victor A. Kramer. New York: HarperCollins, 1996.

———. The Way of Chuang Tzu. New York: New Directions, 1965.

———. *Zen and the Birds of Appetite*. New York: New Directions, 1968.

Merton, Thomas, and Jean Leclercq. *Survival or Prophecy?: The Letters of Thomas Merton and Jean Leclercq*. Ed. Patrick Hart. New York: Farrar, Straus and Giroux, 2002.

Metz, Johann Baptist. *A Passion for God: The Mystical-Political Dimension of Christianity*. Trans. J. Matthew Ashley. Mahwah, N.J.: Paulist Press, 1998.

Mommaers, Paul, and Jan Van Bragt. *Mysticism Buddhist and Christian: Encounters with Jan van Ruusbroec*. New York: Crossroad Publishing Co., 1995.

National Conference of Catholic Bishops. *Economic Justice for All: Pastoral Letter on Catholic Social Teaching and the U.S. Economy*. Washington, D.C.: National Conference of Catholic Bishops, 1986.

O'Collins, Gerald. *Following the Way: Jesus Our Spiritual Director*. London: HarperCollins, 1999.

———. "Jacque Dupuis's Contributions to Interreligious Dialoguc." *Theological Studies* 64:2 (2003) 388–97.

———. *The Second Journey: Spiritual Awareness and the Mid-Life Crisis*. Dublin: Villa Books, 1979.

Ogden, Schubert M. *Is There One True Religion or Are There Many?* Dallas, Texas: Southern Methodist University Press, 1992.

O'Leary, Brian. "The Discernment of Spirits in the Memoriale of Blessed Peter Favre." *The Way* Supplement 35 (1979).

Origen. *Homilies on Joshua*. Trans. Cynthia White. Ed. Barbara J. Bruce. The Fathers of the Church Series, vol. 105. Washington, DC: Catholic University of America Press, 2002.

———. *On First Principles*. Trans. G. W. Butterworth. Gloucester, Mass.: Peter Smith, 1973.

Orsi, Robert A. *Thank You, St. Jude: Women's Devotion to the Patron Saint of Hopeless Causes*. New Haven, Conn.: Yale University Press, 1996.

————. "'Mildred, Is It Fun to Be a Cripple?': The Culture of Suffering in Mid-Twentieth-Century American Catholicism." In *Catholic Lives, Contemporary America*. Ed. Thomas J. Ferraro, 19–64. Durham, N.C.: Duke University Press, 1997.

Panikkar, Raimundo. *The Trinity and the Religious Experience of Man: Icon–Person–Mystery*. Maryknoll, N.Y.: Orbis Books, 1973.

Phan, Peter C. "Multiple Religious Belonging: Opportunities and Challenges for Theology and Church." *Theological Studies* 64:3 (2003) 495–519.

Pieris, Aloysius. "Ignatian Exercises Against a Buddhist Background." *The Way* Supplement 68 (Summer 1990) 98–111.

Polkinghorne, John, and Michael Welker, eds. *The End of the World and the Ends of God: Science and Theology on Eschatology*. Harrisbury, Penn.: Trinity Press International, 2000.

Rahner, Hugo. *Ignatius the Theologian*. Trans. Michael Barry. New York: Herder and Herder, 1968.

Rahner, Karl. "Anonymous Christians." In *Theological Investigations*, vol. 6. London: Darton, Longman & Todd, 1969.

————. "Christianity and the Non-Christian Religions." In *Theological Investigations*, vol. 5. London: Darton, Longman & Todd, 1966.

————. *The Content of Faith: The Best of Karl Rahner's Theological Writings*. Ed. Karl Lehmann and Albert Raffelt. New York: The Crossroad Publishing Co., 1992.

————. *Foundations of Christian Faith: An Introduction to the Idea of Christianity*. New York: The Seabury Press, 1978.

Rahner, Karl, and Paul Imhof. *Ignatius of Loyola*. London: Collins, 1979.

Rakoczy, Susan. "Discernment and Desire." *The Way* 39:3 (1999) 269–80.

Ramsey, Boniface. *John Cassian: The Conferences*. Mahwah, N.J.: Paulist Press, 1997.

Reiser, William. "Adam in Hiding." *Spirituality Today* 38:3 (1986) 242–53.

————. Foreword to *The Spiritual Exercises of Saint Ignatius*, trans. Pierre Wolff. Liguori, Mo.: Triumph, 1997.

————. *Jesus in Solidarity with His People: A Theologian Looks at Mark*. Collegeville, Minn.: The Liturgical Press, 2000.

————. *To Hear God's Word, Listen to the World: The Liberation of Spirituality*. Mahwah, N.J.: Paulist Press, 1997.

————. "The Interior Life of Jesus as the Life of the People of God." In *Spirituality for Ministers*, vol. 2: *Perspectives for the 21ˢᵗ Century*. Ed. Robert J. Wicks, 396–417. Mahwah, N.J.: Paulist Press, 2000.

————. "Looking for the Sign of Jonah: God's Revealing Light Today." *The Way* 38:1 (1998) 9–21.

————. *The Potter's Touch: God Calls Us To Life*. Mahwah, N.J.: Paulist Press, 1981.

————. "Spiritual Literacy: Some Basic Elements." *Lumen Vitae* 42:3 (1987) 329–48.

————. "Truth and Life." *The Way* 19:4 (1979) 251–60.

Rolheiser, Ronald. *The Holy Longing: The Search for a Christian Spirituality.* New York: Doubleday, 1999.

Ruffing, Janet K. *Spiritual Direction: Beyond the Beginnings.* Mahwah, N.J.: Paulist Press, 2000.

————. "Recent Literature and Emerging Issues in the Ministry of Spiritual Direction." *Spiritus* 2:1 (2002) 99–107.

Sanders, E. P. *The Historical Figure of Jesus.* New York: Penguin Books, 1993.

Sands, Bobby. *Bobby Sands: Writings from Prison.* Dublin: Mercier Press Limited, 2001.

Schimmel, Annemarie. *Mystical Dimensions of Islam.* Chapel Hill, N.C.: University of North Carolina Press, 1975.

Schimmel, Solomon. *Wounds Not Healed By Time: The Power of Repentance and Forgiveness.* New York: Oxford University Press, 2002.

Schner, George. "The Appeal to Experience." *Theological Studies* 53:1 (1992) 40–59.

Schütz, John H. *Paul and the Anatomy of Apostolic Authority.* New York: Cambridge University Press, 1975.

Segundo, Juan Luis. *Signs of the Times: Theological Reflections.* Ed. Alfred T. Hennely. Trans. Robert R. Barr. Maryknoll, N.Y.: Orbis Books, 1993.

Sheldrake, Philip. "Ignatius Loyola and Spiritual Direction I." *The Way* 24:4 (1984) 312–19.

————. "Ignatius Loyola and Spiritual Direction II." *The Way* 25:1 (1985) 62–69.

————. *Spirituality and Theology: Christian Living and the Doctrine of God.* Maryknoll, N.Y.: Orbis Books, 1998.

Silf, Margaret. *Wayfaring: A Gospel Journey into Life.* New York: Doubleday, 2001.

Solomon, Robert C. *Spirituality for the Skeptic: The Thoughtful Love of Life.* New York: Oxford University Press, 2002.

Stauffer, Ethelbert. "Theos." In *Theological Dictionary of the New Testament.* Ed. Gerhard Kittel, 3:65–121. Grand Rapids, Mich.: Wm. B. Eerdmans, 1965; 6th printing 1976.

Studzinski, Raymond. *Spiritual Direction and Midlife Development.* Chicago: Loyola University Press, 1985.

Tanner, Norman P., ed. *Decrees of the Ecumenical Councils.* Washington, D.C.: Georgetown University Press, 1990.

Tanquerey, Adolphe. *The Spiritual Life: A Treatise on Ascetical and Mystical Theology.* Westminster, Md.: The Newman Press, 1930.

Terkel, Studs. *Will the Circle Be Broken?: Reflections on Death, Rebirth, and Hunger for a Faith.* New York: New Press, 2001.

Toner, Jules J. *A Commentary on Saint Ignatius' Rules for the Discernment of Spirits: A Guide to the Principles and Practice.* St. Louis, Mo.: Institute of Jesuit Sources, 1982.

———. *Discerning God's Will: Ignatius of Loyola's Teaching on Christian Decision Making.* St. Louis, Mo.: Institute of Jesuit Sources, 1991.

Tracy, David. *Dialogue with the Other: The Inter-Religious Dialogue.* Grand Rapids, Mich.: Wm. B. Eerdmans, 1991.

———. "Fragments: The Spiritual Situation of Our Times." In *God, the Gift, and Postmodernism,* ed. John D. Caputo and Michael Scanlon, 170–81. Bloomington, Ind.: Indiana University Press, 1999.

Trainor, Kevin, ed. *Buddhism: The Illustrated Guide.* New York: Oxford University Press, 2001.

Truth, Sojourner. "The Narrative of Sojourner Truth, a Northern Slave." In *Slave Narratives.* Ed. William L. Andrews and Henry Louis Gates, Jr. New York: Library of America, 2000.

Tylenda, Joseph N., trans. *A Pilgrim's Journey: The Autobiography of Ignatius of Loyola,* rev. ed. San Francisco: Ignatius Press, 2001.

Viviano, Benedict T. "The Gospel According to Matthew." In *The New Jerome Biblical Commentary.* Ed. Raymond E. Brown, Joseph A. Fitzmyer, and Roland E. Murphy, 630–74. Englewood Cliffs, N.J.: Prentice Hall, 1990.

Williams, Rowan. *Lost Icons: Reflections on Cultural Bereavement.* Harrisburg, Pa.: Morehouse Publishing, 2000.

———. *On Christian Theology.* Malden, Mass.: Blackwell Publishers, 2000.

——— *Resurrection: Interpreting the Easter Gospel.* Harrisburg, Penn: Morehouse Publishing, 1994. First published 1982.

Wright, N. T. *Jesus and the Victory of God.* Minneapolis: Fortress Press, 1996.

Wyschogrod, Edith. "Eating the Text, Defiling the Hands: Specters in Arnold Schoenberg's Opera *Moses and Aron.*" In *God, the Gift, and Postmodernism.* Ed. John D. Caputo and Michael J. Scanlon, 245–59. Bloomington, Ind.: Indiana University Press, 1999.

Scriptural Index

Index of Names